A HELPFUL HANDBOOK OF HEBREW HISTORY

A BIBLE-BELIEVING, JESUS-LOVING TAKE

DENNIS TROYER

Copyright © 2024 by Dennis Troyer

All rights reserved.

No part of this book may be reproduced in any form or by any electronic or mechanical means, including information storage and retrieval systems, without written permission from the author, except for the use of brief quotations in a book review. For permissions contact: authors@wisepathbooks.com

Scripture quotations are from the ESV® Bible (The Holy Bible, English Standard Version®), copyright © 2001 by Crossway, a publishing ministry of Good News Publishers. Used by permission. All rights reserved.

The Akkadian Empire map by Simeon Netchev is included with permission from World History Publishing Ltd. (www.worldhistory.org)

The simplified Egypt map by Tina Ross is included with permission from the illustrator. (www.tinaross.ca)

ISBNs:

978-1-959666-25-7 (paperback)
978-1-959666-26-4 (ebook)

Published by:

Wise Path Books
12407 N MoPac Expy #250
Austin, TX 78758

www.wisepathbooks.com

For the glory of God!

CONTENTS

Introduction	9
1. KEY CONCEPTS	17
Dates	17
Agriculture	20
Houses	24
Slavery	26
Slavery in the Ancient Near East	27
Slavery in First Century Roman Empire	30
Covenants	32
2. ANCIENT MAN	37
3. MESOPOTAMIA	49
3100 BC-1761 BC	
Sargon of Akkad	52
Hammurabi	54
4. ANCIENT EGYPT	59
Old Kingdom Egypt	63
Middle Kingdom Egypt	65
5. THE PATRIARCHS AND ANCIENT WARFARE	67
Western Asia in the time of the Patriarchs	73
6. WHO WROTE GENESIS – DEUTERONOMY?	77
7. EGYPT: THE SOJOURN YEARS	83
Gods of Egypt	92
8. TAKING THE LAND OF PROMISE	97
9. ERA OF JUDGES	103
Meanwhile in Israel	110
10. RISE OF MONARCHY IN ISRAEL	115
Solomon	124

11. DIVIDED KINGDOM	129
Assyria	129
Israel and Judah	131
12. JUDAH ON ITS OWN	147
Captivity and Dispersion	156
13. PERSIA GETS CONQUERED	161
14. WESTERN CULTURE	171
Greek Culture	171
Roman Culture	174
15. ISRAEL HAS IT UP TO ITS TONSILS WITH GREEK LEADERSHIP	179
The Maccabean Revolution	182
16. HASMONEAN DYNASTY OF JUDAH	189
17. ROMAN CONQUEST OF JUDEA	195
18. JESUS!	211
Blood of the Martyrs	220
19. RELATIONS BETWEEN ROME AND JUDAH	223
20. ROME AND JUDAH DURING THE TIME OF THE EARLY CHURCH	233
The Spread of the Gospel in the Days Following the Resurrection	236
Colossae / Laodicea / Hierapolis	239
Corinth	240
Ephesus	241
Galatia	244
Philippi	244
Thessalonica	245
Bibliography	247
About the Author	251

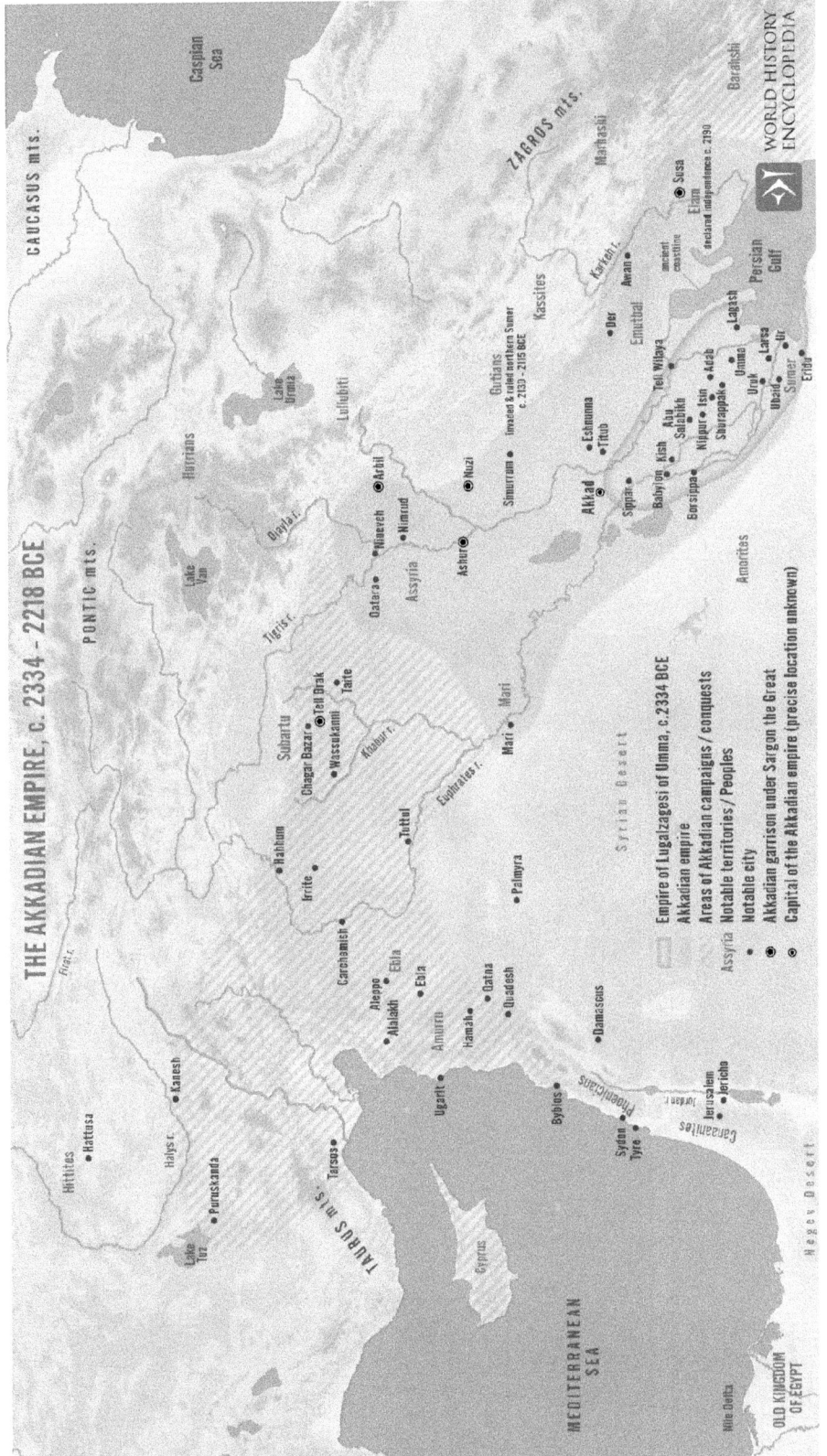

INTRODUCTION

> *The former things I declared of old; they went out from my mouth, and I announced them; then suddenly I did them, and they came to pass. Because I know that you are obstinate, and your neck is an iron sinew and your forehead brass, I declared them to you from of old, before they came to pass I announced them to you, lest you should say, 'My idol did them, my carved image and my metal image commanded them.'*

I could easily overstate the importance of understanding history and culture for your Bible study. You need the Spirit of God to teach you by enlightening His word. You need to draw close to God so He can enlighten your mind. Easily as important as historical and cultural understanding is paying careful attention to context and grammar. Still, even if you know every detail of history, culture, context and grammar, if you do not have God's Spirit guiding you, you will misunderstand the Bible.

That said, understanding the history and culture in the Bible is important. It can greatly help you understand what God is telling you. This is because the Bible was given to people who lived in a world very different from the one you now live in. If you do not understand this background, you could make hilarious mistakes similar to those made by Joseph Smith, founder of Mormonism. In his Book of Mormon, Smith lifted the text of the Sermon on the Mount, King James Translation, and placed it onto the lips of Jesus as He preached to people in the Americas. He had Jesus tell these Americans "Whosoever should compel you to go a mile, go with him twain[1]." This is despite the fact that the Roman Empire had never ruled over the Americas. You see, the practice Jesus referred to was the Roman law that allowed Roman soldiers to force a non-Roman to carry their armor a mile. Jews, such as those being addressed in the Sermon on the Mount, would have been familiar with this practice. Jesus' meaning would be crystal clear in that context.

Consider now the confusion that would have been created had Jesus used such an illustration to people who had never even heard of such a custom. It would have been meaningless. Now, you and I both know that Jesus was a master teacher and would never make such a blunder. Not so Joseph Smith, founder of Mormonism. He had Jesus go on to give instruction about not being like hypocrites who sound a trumpet before themselves in the synagogue[2], even though when the Israelites sailed to the New World[3], according to Smith, Solomon's Temple was still standing[4]. The synagogue was developed as a place of worship in Babylon *after* the destruction of that Temple. Those Israelites would never

---

1. 3 Nephi 12:41
2. 3 Nephi 13:2
3. I am not making this up, I promise.
4. Nephi 1:4

have heard of such a thing. Not even in Joseph Smith's imaginary world.

We can make similar mistakes with the Bible from not knowing history and culture. Most of the time important points go whizzing over our heads; points that the author meant for us to get. Because of this, knowing the history and culture of the world of the Bible can be useful for anyone who wants to understand what is being said. It isn't just for those who geek out about history.

Another major value of this knowledge is that it helps demonstrate the amazing accuracy and authenticity of the Bible. Follow me here. Joseph Smith was not the only "prophet" to make a dog's dinner of Biblical interpretation through lack of historical knowledge. The "prophet" Mohammed seemed to struggle with the notion that Miriam, the sister of Moses and Aaron, was also Mary, mother of Jesus. This is like mistaking Julius Caesar, the famous Roman general and aspiring dictator, for Julio Cesar Chavez, the best pound- for-pound boxer of his era. Mohammed peppered the Koran with this error[5]. You see, you can expect a book written by men to have error. The Bible, on the other hand, despite being written by multiple authors over 1500 years, is free of error. This can be seen when you look at how it lacks historical or cultural mistakes. You would expect, if you understand this issue, for such a document to abound with massive, hilarious mistakes. If the Bible were authored by mere men, it should be child's play to poke holes all throughout it. Instead, all of the events and practices found in the Bible fit into the actual history of the world we live in.

"Wait just a minute, my Bible thumping friend," you might

---

5. Surah 3: 35-45, Surah 19:28, Surah 66:12

reply[6]. "What about all of the ludicrously impossible things that go on constantly in the Bible?"

This is an important point to consider. Any honest historian has to confront the fact that the historical record does not abound in miraculous happenings. In the real world, people who die generally stay that way on a permanent basis. There is no question that we live in a world of natural laws that seem to function pretty regularly. How does the responsible historian, faced with this difficulty, continue arguing for the Bible?

First, the Bible claims to be divinely inspired by God. God intervening in the world is the entire premise. That miraculous things do not generally occur is rather the point. Anybody can claim to speak for God, but not just anybody can suspend the natural order of the universe. Jesus demonstrated that He is the Son of God with power by His resurrection from the dead[7]. It is a sign and wonder. That it is not the normal way of things and that nobody can reproduce it in a laboratory is precisely the point. God is behind this! Look, miracles!

It is also worth noting that while it may seem that life for people in the Bible is nothing but a nonstop supernatural wonder fest, this is just because those are the things being discussed. The narrative of the Bible covers from creation to the First Century AD. Thousands of years pass, and for most of them no miracles are recorded. After creation we have a spate of signs in Egypt in the Fifteenth Century BC with Moses, a couple in the next century after a forty year pause as God drove out Israel's enemies, a smattering in Canaan during the kingdom of Israel by Elijah and Elisha and then the ones by Jesus and the Apostles in the First Century AD. There were some other occurrences but of the "previ-

---

6. If you have not yet been convinced of the historical reliability of the Bible.
7. Romans 1:4

barren woman now gets pregnant" variety. Really, most places saw no obvious miracles and there were hundreds of years between the times. Obviously supernatural miracles were by no means normal occurrences in Biblical times.

There is another interesting value to this historical and cultural accuracy of the Bible. In order to discount the prophecy found in the Bible, critics try to claim that these predictions were made after the fact. You see, the prophecies in the Bible are very specific and there would be no other way to argue against divine authorship. Critics have a worldview that discounts supernatural events like the parting of the Red Sea or the resurrection from the dead of our Lord and Savior. Everyone agrees that these are not ordinary events. Believers argue that God is demonstrating His power. Critics argue that since such things do not *normally* occur, they cannot. Divine foretelling of the future would smash the critics' worldview. A world where God accurately describes the future is a world where the miraculous might just occur.

The problem critics have to face is the accuracy of the Bible when it comes to history and culture of places far away both physically and in time from their supposed later authors. By understanding this accuracy, we are able to see the proof left for us by God in His word of its divine origin.

Contrary to what some people seem to think, the past is not all the same over the millennia. Culture changes over the years, as do practices. Technology develops, governments change. The Pagan Scandinavians of the Ninth Century accepted Christianity and crusaded against the Pagan Balts in the Thirteenth Century, partially at least to force them to convert. Armies go from using chariots to having people ride on the backs of the horses. There are real differences between even neighboring groups.

The writers of history in ancient times had serious problems. While a group might keep careful records of the reigns of their own rulers and events in their own realms, they often failed horribly with events in other nations or events at times other than that of the one recording it. They have mythological figures in the past before their chroniclers began keeping records, with wild events unique to their tales. I hope I am not spilling the beans when I tell you that they did not have the sort of information-rich society where you could look up the history of neighboring peoples on Google.

You can read in Roman histories how Romulus and Remus squabbled over the rule of the city of Rome[8]. They describe the succession of rulers, and at some point you get to real people. Another example is Ragnar Lothbrok. He, if the Icelandic Chronicles are to be believed, spent his early days slaying giant serpents and rescuing trapped princesses. He swanked about doing the Danish version of the adventures of Hercules in a way that no historian would take even slightly seriously. Later in life, he raided England where he was killed. His sons dropped by and took their revenge. The problem: there is record of his son, Ivar the Boneless, leading a great heathen army in conquest of English kingdoms. Ragnar's sons were real people. They had to have a father. Ivar's real name was Ivar Ragnarsson. Where does the mythology stop, and the real history begin? This is all too often the muck of non-modern history.

The upshot is that you would not expect Fifth Century BC scribes in Jerusalem or Babylon to be privy to detailed historical and cultural information of Fifteenth Century BC Egypt. You can't. You would also not expect Jews from the First Century BC to know much detail about Sixth Century Babylon. It just would not happen. Presence of historical and cultural accuracy of other

---

8. Remus: "I think we should call it Reme." Romulus, drawing his sword: "I have a better idea."

places and times in Scripture will show you that arguments of late authorship are baseless. In short, this accuracy demonstrates that the prophecy did predict future events by establishing when and where it was made. True prophecy, not after the fact, no matter the shreds this makes of the naturalistic worldview.

There are ever so many ways to see the truth of Scripture. The timeless truth that gets to the real root causes of man's condition. The overwhelming beauty of the ideas expressed. The moral excellence of the precepts of God that excel the moral standards of all ages of men. All of these things tell us that the Bible is the word of God. My hope is that this book will build my reader up by helping to demonstrate that truth through the study of history.

Now there are many ways to go about the task of fitting the Scriptural record in with the history of the rest of the world. There is considerable debate about the precise dates of Biblical events. To a certain extent these discussions are important. Failure to take a careful note of the years mentioned in the Bible can lead to misdating that places Biblical events in times where they did not occur and has Israelites in places that they should not be. My assumption, when I go about the task, is that if I take the Bible seriously there will be corroborating evidence of the Biblical record in archeology and historical records.

The task of figuring out dates is difficult, involving a great deal of study and work. There are passages of Scripture over which people disagree as to interpretation. There are sometimes multiple passages that must be harmonized so that each passage is interpreted rightly. Some people who are also committed to Scripture will have timelines that differ from mine in some ways. It is possible they are right. I am giving my best account based on my knowledge. The Bible is the word of God. My book is not. Feel free to disagree without any fear of divine judgment[9].

You will also notice a list of books at the end. These are the historians who instructed me through their writings and on whose shoulders I stand. Most people, normal people, will hopefully enjoy our quick jaunt through history. If you are like me and want to know more, I can recommend these books. Their authors have done the hard work and research to explain all of these things in depth. Even though they are all far more knowledgeable than I am, I do not agree with every one of them on every point. This is okay because they often do not agree with each other.

---

9. Except on the date of the Exodus. Indignation and wrath on every soul of man who holdeth to the Thirteenth Century Exodus.

1

KEY CONCEPTS

Dates

> *For inquire, please, of bygone ages, and consider what the fathers have searched out. For we are but of yesterday and know nothing, for our days on earth are a shadow.*

When assigning dates to historical occurrences, I like to use an approach that assumes that once I understand what the Bible is saying, it will fit because it is true. I use the chronology set out by Scripture and then use everything I can find to figure out how the Bible's chronology fits in with the histories of other people who maintained records. They should mesh because reality is like that. The truth will fit like a glove.

Unfortunately, while the Bible is true, other sources are often interpreted for us by people who would be embarrassed to report that they match what the Bible says. While the Bible is constantly being vindicated as knowledge grows, these experts who disagree with Scripture take comfort in the fact that they at the very least get to be right initially.

Figuring out dates in the Bible is more complicated than you might think. Most of the passages are either of the "how long a king ruled" or "this thing happened this many years after that thing" variety. You can make a pretty good Biblical chronology, but the challenge is to synchronize that chronology with our dating system that we use today. Fortunately, other ancient peoples also were able to keep records that included chronologies.

The Egyptian chronologies are not optimal. The Egyptians' religion does not allow for more than one god-incarnate-Pharaoh at the same time. As a result, when rule in Egypt is divided into two or more kingdoms, the Egyptian chronology tends to number them sequentially and make believe that they ruled one after another instead of simultaneously. This can lead to the illusion of long ages of rule when the time period is actually much shorter.

Another problem that the Egyptians have is their Pharaohs' tendency to claim every accomplishment they think they can get away with. This makes it hard to pin down which one did what or when one of those beautiful structures was actually built. This sort of thing is why we can no longer be entirely sure who actually united Upper and Lower Egypt.

The Assyrians' chronology, though, is everything an ancient chronology should be, in my opinion. Okay, so they spin events to make things look like they are ever victorious, so they aren't perfect. Instead of having to tromp around scanning monuments for information like in Egypt, they kept tablets with events from the year. You just grab the tablet for the year you are interested in and there are the events. Fair warning, though, they did not use our current dating system so you can't just grab tablets looking for the cuneiform version of 1234 BC.

The main reason the Assyrian chronicles are so useful is that they record astronomical occurrences. When they record an eclipse, we can use astronomical software to figure out exactly when, using our dating system, that occurred in their location. Even though they did not use our dating system, you can line their years up to ours using this data.

With that in mind, we have record of Jehu of Israel paying tribute to Shalmanezer IV in his eighteenth year. Shalmanezer IV's eighteenth year is 841 BC. We also have record of the battle of Qarqar, featuring Ahab of Israel in the sixth year of Shalmanezer III, which is 853 BC. Sennacherib records when he came against Hezekiah of Judah, which corresponds to 701 BC.

With these dates in hand, we can attach dates to the chronology of the kings of Israel and Judah. We can work to the date of the destruction of Jerusalem by Nebuchadnezzar. Even more importantly for our purposes, we can use the chronology of the kings to work back to the reign of Solomon. Once we have the date for Solomon, we have hit pay dirt for following the Biblical chronology to dating the patriarchs, Exodus from Egypt, and conquest of Canaan.

Solomon began the construction of the first Temple in his fourth year, four hundred eighty years after the Exodus[1]. We can date this to 966 BC, giving us an Exodus in 1446 BC. Israel is in Egypt for four hundred thirty years[2] so Jacob and his seventy souls came down in 1876 BC. Jacob was one hundred thirty years old when he was introduced to Pharaoh[3], so he was born in 2006 BC. Isaac was sixty when Jacob was born[4] so Isaac was born in 2066 BC. As you should know, Abraham had to wait until he was one

---

1. I Kings 6:1
2. Exodus 12:41
3. Genesis 47:9
4. Genesis 25:26

hundred to have his son Isaac[5], which has Abram being born in 2166 BC. Abram was called to leave Haran when he was seventy-five[6], which makes his initial entry into the Promised Land 2091 BC.

Now the chronicles of the Kings of Israel and Judah are complicated beyond the scope of this book. There are accession years that are included in some chronologies and not others. There are periods where more than one king is ruling, either because of a co-regency or a divided kingdom. The laborious work of ironing all of this out was done by a scholar named Edwin Thiele. If you want to know how all of that works out, go buy his book; he explains it well. It is a smidge more academic, but this is the price one pays for deeper understanding.

Agriculture

> *Now the angel of the LORD came and sat under the terebinth at Ophrah, which belonged to Joash the Abiezrite, while his son Gideon was beating out wheat in the winepress to hide it from the Midianites. And the angel of the LORD appeared to him and said to him, "The LORD is with you, O mighty man of valor."*

One thing that will no doubt be strange for the modern reader of the Bible is the agrarian society it portrays. After all, today we can obtain a meal for less than the cost of an hour's hired labor. Today most people live in cities, and we have a wide variety of professions. Between farm machinery and agricultural technology such

---

5. Genesis 21:5
6. Genesis 12:4

as fertilizers and improved crop strains, it takes far fewer people to grow the food necessary to feed all of the people. This allows most people to do other things than work full time to produce the food that they need to survive.

In ancient times most people worked full time producing food. They might watch sheep, or they might grow grain, but their job was to produce enough food to feed themselves and their household. The reason for this is that people had a hard time producing much more food than would feed the people needed to raise it. There was not a lot of food left over for people who did other jobs. People who lived near rivers could be more productive and so those societies were able to have more people specialize in jobs other than food production.

There are a number of important ramifications from this fact. First, since fewer people specialized in producing goods, most people had to make many of their own goods. While not watching the sheep, a wife would need to know how to spin the wool into yarn or thread and then to weave it into cloth. Men would need to know how to build buildings or cut hides to make tents. Because of this, people tended to be more self-sufficient in that they made most of what they used.

In another way people were less self-sufficient. They needed to cooperate at certain times of the year to plant and harvest crops. They often worked together as a community to make sure everyone was able to get all of the harvest in. They had to defend each other from attack by raiders or wild animals. Less specialization also meant fewer men could be professional soldiers. This meant that the men who raised crops or watched sheep were also often the ones who went to war in ancient society.

You will find a mixed sort of agriculture being practiced in the Promised Land. They grew wheat and barley in fields. This composed the main article of food and where they would get most of their calories. To grow grains, they had to plow the fields with the help of animals; most of the time they would use oxen. Oxen are bulls that have been castrated when they were young. They are more docile than bulls but still large and able to do work. Farmers would often use a wooden collar, called a yoke, which would connect two oxen together. The plow would be pulled by the oxen while a man walked behind.

Once the grain had grown, it was cut down with long curved blades called sickles or scythes. The tall stalks of grain were then gathered together. This was called reaping.

Wheat and barley were actually sorts of tall grass. After the grass was cut down, the farmers needed to get the edible seeds separated from the inedible stems. They would accomplish this by threshing the grain. Threshing was where they would knock the seeds off of the stems either by beating them or driving a sledge over them. Sometimes this sledge would be pulled by a cow. After the seeds were no longer attached, the grain would be winnowed. This was accomplished by going where there was a strong wind and tossing the mixture up in the air. The nonedible stems, or chaff, would be blown away while the seeds would fall back down to be collected.

They had trees that produced figs and olives. Figs they simply ate, so having those was a lot like having an apple tree. Olives, though, were mostly used to produce oil they used to fuel lamps. Not everyone could produce oil so this was a luxury good that could be sold for money. Trees like these were valuable and would have to be planted years before they started to produce. They required water so they needed to be carefully tended. It was useful to have them in the hilly areas because much of the land was not flat enough for growing grain. This will be particularly significant when we look at the hilly lands throughout Palestine.

Another option for hilly land was raising livestock. Animals could graze on land that would not support the growing of grain. One could also get meat, and fiber for weaving. Many farmers had some animals as well.

They also raised vines that produced grapes. These were valued because with them they could produce wine. Like trees, these vines also required careful tending. The fruit was crushed and then fermented to produce wine. The press to crush the grapes was an area often cut into the rock where they would tread on the grapes. There were channels that allowed the juice to flow out into another area where it could collect.

Another agricultural processing item often found low in altitude was the mill. This was where large stone wheels were rolled over the grain to grind it into flour. These millstones had to be very large and heavy to do their work. Millstones and winepresses were often used by the community as a whole. Each household would bring its goods to be processed.

People in Canaan tended many sorts of animals but the most numerous were sheep. Sheep are domesticated animals because without a shepherd they would quickly die in the wild. This is because sheep have their stupid dials set to eleven. They panic whenever they see a predator and can be killed without even touching them as they will run around until they have a heart attack. They need to be led to food or water. They will roll over and be unable to stand back up. They are like a Golden Corral Buffet for predators.

The job of shepherd did not carry the positive connotations we have given it in the Christian world. It was a nasty job where you got to spend freezing nights and sweltering days with smelly, stupid sheep. It was the job that was given to those who were low on the pecking order.

The reason shepherds get so much play in the Bible is that sheep are stupid and will die swiftly without their shepherd. They are totally dependent on their shepherd for survival. He leads them to food and protects them from danger. There are many warm bodies but the only brain that really works is in the head of the shepherd. Keep this in mind the next time you read the Twenty-Third Psalm.

Houses

> *And the LORD said unto Noah, Come thou and all*
> *thy house into the ark; for thee have I seen righteous*
> *before me in this generation.*

Now, how did Noah fit his house on the ark along with all of those animals? I hope you know that the word house has more than one meaning. In this section I want to talk about the term in the sense of a family unit. Today we still have these sorts of houses. The House of Windsor is the ruling family of the United Kingdom of Great Britain and Northern Ireland. This sort of house today is associated with nobility or royalty. It has hereditary lands and properties and a title for the head of the family. In the United States particularly, we have gotten away from this sort of thing. Right after high school we scoot out the door to college or career. Even if we do live at home with the parents, it's generally a temporary thing until the financial crisis abates. We live in small nuclear families and either own businesses or work for wages.

In the early days of mankind houses were family, financial and governmental units all combined. At the core, in most cases, a house was a prosperous family. This was not a little nuclear family like we normally have today but a larger clan. It could include the head, his six sons and their families. It might even include the younger brothers of the head with their descendants. With the number of children that people had in the past, it would represent a sizable number in many cases. Abram's tiny family, just himself and his wife after he separated from Lot, underscores just how amazing God's promise was that he would make a mighty nation of him.

If you are at all familiar with the Genesis narrative of the life of Abraham, you know that there were more people in his house than two. Sarai had a female servant Hagar. When Lot was captured, Abram armed over three hundred of his men and joined his Amorite allies to rescue Lot. These people were also members of the house, but they were not family. Today we would refer to them as slaves. I will talk about the similarities and differences that exist between ancient and more recent sorts of slavery in another section. For our purposes now, let it suffice that there are considerable differences. When Abram thought he was going to die childless, he said that his servant Eliezer of Damascus would inherit[7] everything he had. In a similar way Joseph, the second most powerful man in Egypt, was a slave to Pharaoh. The reason for this was that though they were not family, they were members of the house.

Now the house would have assets that allowed its people to produce a living. Perhaps it was land that they could farm or, in Abram's case, a large herd of animals. From this property all of the members of the house drew their livelihood in proportion. The head would get the most, the lowest ranking slave what he was allotted. Everyone in the house cooperated to accomplish the work as well. Each had his or her role. Working for wages was far less common. Most people were members of a house, either family or servants. People did work for wages at times, but that was not nearly so common as today.

---

7. Genesis 15:2-3

In addition to being a family unit, the house was like a modern company. You can look at it that way too if it helps. In that case the head had the controlling interest while the lesser members were shareholders with shares comparable to their position in the house. Instead of money, the employees were paid in their stock. It was like an employee-owned corporation, with the caveat that management, which normally consisted of a man known as the head, had a controlling interest. All labor was for the profit of the company that all had a vested interest in maintaining since it provided the livelihood for everyone. Because the economy was more agrarian, household production was normally about producing the food necessary for survival.

Most houses were smaller groups made up primarily of extended family members. Some houses were much larger. You will learn in the section on early civilization that there were priestly houses that dominated the early cities. The first kings, called lugals, were just heads of powerful houses, able to mobilize many men for battle to defend their cities. You can see then how this societal structure formed the basis of noble and royal houses. These houses today are just the last vestiges of a way of organizing society that has existed for thousands of years.

By understanding the concept of house, you can better understand many of the historical situations and analogies presented in the Bible and so better understand the Bible.

Slavery

> *Here there is not Greek and Jew, circumcised and uncircumcised, barbarian, Scythian,* **slave,** *free; but Christ is all, and in all.*

Oddly enough, when someone mentions slavery, what comes to the minds of most Americans is not the sort of slavery practiced today, such as human trafficking or children spending their lives at sea in Indochina catching fish to produce dog food. Instead we think of slavery from the eighteenth and nineteenth centuries in the Americas. This is because this sort of slavery is taught in school almost to the complete exclusion of all other sorts. Slavery has been practiced all over the world since the dawn of recorded history.

My purpose is not to educate my reader about slavery throughout history, but to explain what it was like in the times that the Bible speaks of. This is quite enough for any chapter anyhow. Even in the period stretching between the Patriarchs and the First Century Roman Empire there were considerable variations in the practice.

Slavery in the Ancient Near East

In the previous section on houses, I promised to treat on slavery in more detail and it is in the context of the houses of the ancient world that I will begin this look at slavery. The fact is that for some members of the household, it is debatable if they would even fit our definition of slaves at all. Most members of a household would not want to leave since they obtained their livelihood from the house. They had been associated with that house for generations and even though they were not related to the head of the family they had a place in the house. For many it was more like being part of a cooperative than being property.

Abram had three hundred herdsmen that he called on for battle. He did not have warriors or guards. There was nobody to coerce their labor. If three hundred herdsmen wanted to no longer watch his sheep, they would have been able to find a way. No, these men respected and loved the head of their house and prospered as the house did. Another example was Eliezer of Damascus. He walked out of Abraham's presence with camels loaded down with gold and jewelry. He did not take the money and run; he went out and did his work for the house by finding a wife for the heir. His mission accomplished, he returned from Syria with Rebecca. Most of the members of these households were loyal to their house and would have hated to lose their position in it.

As you can see, most of these people were also not purchased or sold. They belonged to the house and the house belonged to the head of the house. Technically you could consider them property after a fashion, but the lack of coercion makes it hard to really put them in the class of slave as we would normally think of it. On the other hand, they couldn't just leave. Even if nobody would stop them, they would not be able to make it on the outside. Survival required cooperative effort in the ancient world. The lone wolf died. If you ran off from your master, others would be hesitant to take you in. Neighboring groups would be more likely to view you with either distrust or outright hostility. The likely outcomes would be starvation or being enslaved by others with a new position on the bottom of the hierarchy.

Now being sold into slavery did happen. Many times, people would sell themselves when they could not produce enough food to feed themselves. Becoming a slave was preferable to allowing your family to starve to death. In this case you would find a house that was prospering and had food to spare. You could then trade your labor for the food to sustain your life, and perhaps that of your family.

Another way was to be enslaved in war. Taking people as slaves instead of killing them was common in the ancient world. Male slaves taken this way could help with the work but posed a security threat since they might do violence if they escaped. Female slaves were less of a danger and had the added benefit that men could get mates in this manner. Taking war brides from the enemy was not uncommon and was considered a normal sort of loot to take from battle. While this sort of thing seems abhorrent to our modern sensibilities, it is just how things were in the ancient world.

While slaves in the Americas during the eighteenth and nineteenth centuries almost universally were of low social status, this was not always the case in the ancient world. The high servants in a powerful house would enjoy very high social standing. In the extreme case of a royal house, the highest slave could serve as prime minister of a kingdom or even empire. Slaves could be trusted to have no ambitions of their own and were considered less of a threat to the ruler when given power. Joseph and Daniel in the Bible are both examples of slaves of extremely high social standing.

This has obvious ramifications for how you understand passages that mention slavery in the Bible. Slaves are always to be obedient to their masters, but they are not automatically degraded or on the bottom of society. High slaves could enjoy more wealth and privilege than the heads of some households. This explains how we can be slaves of Christ yet simultaneously seated with Him on high as joint heirs.

There was also a sort of slavery that could be called national slavery. This was when a vassal suzerain treaty[8] required the vassal to provide labor. In this case the vassal would have to provide slave labor to the suzerain. The laborers were enslaved by their own government and sent to work. This did not necessarily mean that they were not paid, but they were forced to work. One example of this is the Children of Israel in Egypt. The Egyptians sent word to

---

8. For more on sorts of treaties see chapter 6.

the Israelites about how many bricks they were to provide to fulfill their obligations. In this case the whole nation was enslaved.

Another example would be the Gibeonites who were made to send members of their cities to work as hewers of wood and drawers of water[9] for the Israelites once they were in the Promised Land. The Gibeonites continued to rule their cities but were forced to provide labor in perpetuity in return for military protection.

Slavery in First Century Roman Empire

One could become a slave in First Century Rome in a number of ways. The first and most common was to belong to a conquered enemy of Rome. Whole cities that defied Rome were sold into slavery. Provinces and cities that rebelled against Rome also often had large portions sold into slavery. Many Jews entered slavery from the periodic unrest and rebellion in Jerusalem.

Another common way to enter slavery in First Century Rome was to be poor. People who could not pay their debts could be sold into slavery to satisfy their debts. Some would sell themselves into slavery to avoid starvation if they found themselves impoverished.

Because children had no rights in First Century Rome, they could be sold into slavery if their parents chose to do so. Some children entered slavery because their parents abandoned them and someone else found them and thus owned them as slaves to sell or keep.

Another way to enter slavery was to be sentenced to it as punishment for a crime. Roman justice had little difficulty taking your life, liberty or happiness if you were found guilty of a crime.

---

9. Joshua 9:27

Often times this resulted in slavery to the state, a way into very undesirable jobs.

Some plantations that were worked by large groups of slaves did exist in Italy. These latifundia or spacious estates were often used to produce luxury crops like olives and grapes. Here could be found the closest thing to the sort of mass agricultural labor camps as might have been found in antebellum southeastern states.

Some slaves, often times Greeks, would be used as tutors for the children of Roman citizens. Because Greeks were often educated and schooled in the literature and culture of Greece, they were desirable for the education of Roman youth. Greeks were also educated in rhetoric, which was desirable for Roman youth, particularly those from upper class families.

Slaves were very common in rich Roman households as servants. They performed many specialized roles and served also as status symbols. A wealthy and powerful family could display its standing by having many slaves. Slaves could serve in menial serving roles from personal attendants to cooks. Educated slaves were common and could be used to manage household affairs, freeing up leisure time for their masters.

Even those not of the upper classes would sometimes have slaves that would help them. It was not uncommon to see slaves working alongside their masters in all manner of trade.

Things in Rome could, however, be profoundly worse for a slave as well. Most of the time this was when they were made slaves of the Roman government itself. Somebody had to go underground and mine metals and salt. Gladiator shows needed people to spill their blood for entertainment purposes. Slaves had no protection from cruel punishments. People could be just as nasty back then as they are today so that sort of thing did happen.

Slavery in First Century Rome was not always permanent.

Slaves were commonly freed or manumitted. In the case of debt slaves, they could be ransomed for the amount of their debt. They were normally paid some wage, so they could save up to pay themselves out. Slaves freed in Rome became citizens of Rome[10], allowing them a number of rights. This was common in the testaments of Romans upon their deaths.

Relations between slaves and masters were often cordial with slaves serving as members of their master's house. Household slaves were often regarded with benevolence by their masters and slaves often were loyal to their master and his interests. An example of this were the slaves in Caesar's household. Some of Caesar's higher slaves were more influential and powerful than the vast majority of Roman citizens.

Even with all of these positive features, the law was never on the side of slaves. Even once freed they could never hope to rise high in society in their own name. The stench of lowly beginnings marred their chances in society. Slaves that fled from or displeased their masters could be put to death. In such cases it was not uncommon for escaped slaves to seek the anonymity of Rome. Rome had a massive population with a regular bread dole. It was easy to lose yourself in the crowd and survive undetected in the slums.

Covenants

> *When Abram was ninety-nine years old the L*ORD *appeared to Abram and said to him, "I am God Almighty; walk before me, and be blameless, that I may make my covenant between me and*

---

10. See the section on Roman Culture.

you, and may multiply you greatly." Then Abram fell on his face. And God said to him, "Behold, my covenant is with you, and you shall be the father of a multitude of nations. No longer shall your name be called Abram, but your name shall be Abraham, for I have made you the father of a multitude of nations. I will make you exceedingly fruitful, and I will make you into nations, and kings shall come from you. And I will establish my covenant between me and you and your offspring after you throughout their generations for an everlasting covenant, to be God to you and to your offspring after you. And I will give to you and to your offspring after you the land of your sojournings, all the land of Canaan, for an everlasting possession, and I will be their God."

A covenant is a solemn, formal pledge or promise. It is like the legal contract of the ancient world. While there may be many things one might call a covenant, what I would like to talk about now is the sort that was used as a treaty between rulers. A powerful king could defeat his neighbor and then with his aid subjugate other nearby cities. This was how powerful rulers were able to form empires in the ancient Near East.

Most kings in the ancient world ruled over a single city. More power could be acquired by a king by binding another king to service through a covenant. Often this sort of covenant could be forced on another through war. It might not even be necessary to do any actual fighting. The goal was to get another king to submit himself and his city to you as your vassal. The one who was the ruler in this case would be called the suzerain. Unsurprisingly, this sort of covenant was known as a vassal suzerain treaty.

The suzerain and the vassal each agreed to certain terms in the covenant. In addition to not burning the vassal's city down, the suzerain would provide protection if the vassal were attacked by some other party. In return the vassal would be submissive and provide what the suzerain wanted. Often this meant that the vassal would lead troops in support of the suzerain at his command. It could also just mean that the vassal had to send troops to serve in the army. The vassal could also be required to provide tribute in goods or in laborers who would work for the suzerain. As we go over the history, it is important to understand who are vassals to whom. It will affect who they side with in war.

These covenants were not always kept. The balance of power between two mighty suzerains could be shifted by getting one of their opponent's vassals to switch sides. It was also not uncommon for vassals to grow weary of paying tribute. Then they might make alliances with other vassals or another suzerain and throw off their covenant. Either way, it was quite common for these covenants to be broken, particularly by the vassals.

To try to limit this sort of thing, most ancient covenants contained stipulations where the vassals bound themselves to be cursed by their own gods if they should break their covenant. If fear of gods was not sufficient, breaking a covenant was almost certainly grounds for a military response from the suzerain. A successful reprisal by the suzerain could result in anything from a raid to replacement of the king and reinstatement of the covenant, to burning of the city with enslavement of the population.

There are several reasons that I am bringing this covenant thing up. First and foremost, there are covenants between man and God in the Bible. Naturally, God is the suzerain who provides protection for his vassals. As vassals there are stipulations of tribute and expectations of loyalty. Paying attention to the stipulations of the covenant in each case can help the careful Bible student understand what is being communicated in the passage.

Second, not all covenants are the same. Some sorts of covenant were used centuries after others. Much can be made of this sort of information by historians with their eyes on the ball when dating the covenant in question.

2

ANCIENT MAN

*When I look at your heavens, the work of your fingers,
the moon and the stars, which you have set in
place, what is man that you are mindful of him,
and the son of man that you care for him?
Yet you have made him a little lower than the heavenly
beings and crowned him with glory and honor. You
have given him dominion over the works of your
hands; you have put all things under his feet, all
sheep and oxen, and also the beasts of the field, the
birds of the heavens, and the fish of the sea, whatever passes along the paths of the seas.*

Long ago, the evolutionist's myth starts, people were more like the common simian ancestor. They lived in caves and their hobbies included figuring out fire and how to make a stick pointy so they could stab something. They spent their days pounding rocks together and grunting unintelligibly. Their lowered brows held brains too tiny to come up with a more advanced way of life. All too often we buy this whole story. I know I did. Maybe we get this idea from the images we are fed of cave men wearing tiger skin unitards with a club in one hand and the hair of an unconscious woman, which he is dragging behind him, in the other. This image, however, is as mythological as that of elves or orcs. One of the first misconceptions that I believe it is vital to do away with right off the bat is the idea that ancient people were somehow less intelligent than we are today.

To understand the ancient people, you first need to cast your mind to a different place. Imagine the most remote place you have ever been. You can look as far as you want and there is no sign of human habitation. There are no grocery stores. No stores of any kind. There are no roads. There are no restaurants. There is nobody to call if you need food or shelter. You couldn't call if there were because there are no phones. You and you only can provide yourself and your family food, shelter, clothing, and protection.

Suddenly what the weather is like, what animals are running around and what plants grow become matters of life or death. You have to figure out how to make use of what you find to build a stable life. Not only do you have to find food, but you need to have a plan for what to do if you don't find any. If you are running short on food, who has to go hungry? If you need to move to find food, what do you do if the place you go already has people there?

There is no national or state government to punish people who rob or murder you. How big your family is becomes vitally important. A man with six grown sons has more to say in disputes than a man with none[1]. Staying close to relatives for protection is simple survival. Having friends, and who they are, can be a matter of similar importance. It is in this world, with far fewer people in it and almost none of our modern conveniences, that we must begin.

---

1. Psalm 127:5

In this environment people had three basic strategies for survival: hunting and gathering, herding, and farming. These strategies took into account the different conditions in which people lived. Often people would use combinations of these strategies for survival. Just because you started raising corn did not mean you couldn't also have a cow and go fishing on Saturday.

Now, I would never argue that people never lived in caves or wore skins as clothing. I am just saying that people who did so were not doing so because of tiny brains. In the distant past, population levels were much lower. When population levels are low enough, you can get enough food to feed yourself and your family by hunting the animals and fishing. You can also gather berries and roots that you find. There would be no reason to work to create more since the land provides all you need. Clothing would come from the same animals you hunt. With such a lifestyle, it would be necessary to move around a bit to find more animals and plants to eat, so building a permanent dwelling would not make a lot of sense. Portable dwellings or found shelter, like caves, would be the order of the day for such a lifestyle.

How many people, do you think, would rather live this way than work forty hours or, let's face it, often far more, every week? Quite a few, I am willing to bet. Is it because they have tiny brains in sloped foreheads? No. As long as there are not too many people for the land, this is a reasonable way to live. It is not burdensome with work and there is not much need for technological innovations. Need, I have heard, is the mother of invention.

The difficulty is that people confuse technology with intelligence. This is the same sort of arrogant assumption that led Europeans to assume that the American Indians of the US, First Nations of Canada and natives of South America were stupid primitives. Ask yourself, did you invent the computer or automobile? Logically, how could you equate the technology that is given to you with intelligence then? Now, I am not saying that there are not technologies that enhance intelligence. Large vocabularies and reading books enhance the cognitive development of children. Education will make you smarter. My point is that if you were to take a child from these early days and give them the same education, you could expect similar results.

There are people living "primitive" lives to this day in areas of the world where population levels are low enough. In the Amazon rainforest and on islands people are still living off of the bounty of the land and water. These people are not idiots or primitive missing-link ape men. They are intelligent people who have not yet found the need to live a different lifestyle. I would contend that this is true throughout history. People in the past were intelligent and capable, even though some did live simply off of the land. This is a product of low population levels instead of lack of intelligence.

Sometimes there is just not enough in nature to feed everyone in an area. One option is to kill people until the competition for resources becomes easier again. This results in tribal warfare and has been employed by hunter-gatherer groups all over the world. It isn't nice but it is effective. Another is to increase the food supply. Two methods have been used by people throughout history to do this: tending animals for food and products like milk, wool or eggs and tending plants for later consumption.

Tending animals, or herding, has a number of advantages. You can herd on ground that is too dry for growing crops. Your diet is rich in protein. Having a herd means you know where your food supply is. The animal can be chosen for the products it offers including milk, wool or hide. Housing can be made from the hide; clothing from the hide, hair or wool. You do have to move around quite a bit, like the hunter-gatherer. This can be a good thing in times of drought; you can leave to better lands until the rains come. It is a great deal more work than hunting and gathering but can support more people for the amount of land used. In the event that herders come into conflict with hunter-gatherers, the larger population of the herders means that they will usually be able to push them off of the land or absorb them.

Agriculture is the raising of plants for food, usually grains. This way of life offers the most food for an area of land. This means that a given area of land can support the most people. The abundance of food means that people who live by agriculture will have the most resistance to famine because they can have large amounts of stored food.

Agriculture has its downsides too. It is hard work. It means long hours for many hands to plant, tend and harvest crops. It only works when there is plenty of water. You need a river or plenty of rain[2]. It would only work in limited areas because of this. Many people would crowd into an area and competition for good growing areas could cause conflict. If there is not enough water, all the work is for nothing. Lack of rain in one year, causing a failed crop, could be compensated for with stored grain. Prolonged drought could be disastrous. Ironically, agriculture's short term famine resistance turns into a liability in cases of long-term loss of water resources. An example of such is the Indus River valley civilization in modern day Pakistan that seems to have fallen because of a change in the course of the river.

Agriculture also allows people to stay in one place, so building permanent dwellings would be the norm. What the houses are made of will vary with what is available. Often times dried mud, wood and stone are used. It becomes normal to live like we do today, in community with neighbors. The drawback is that moving

---

2. Unless you are from Central Mexico. Then you can do as you like without much rain.

around just is not in the cards. This means that if the grain does stop growing for whatever reason, starting up somewhere else is difficult and more food is months in the future at the least. Lastly, moving is a defense against raids and attacks by those who want to take the food or land or even both. This competition for the lands where crops could grow makes it necessary for cooperation for defense as well.

When enough really successful farmers live in close proximity and cooperate in planting, harvesting, and improving the land with irrigation, enough grain can be produced that not everyone needs to work as farmers. Instead, some can specialize in other work. From builders to administrators and from soldiers to priests, specialization moves the settlement into what is known as civilization. This just means that they are able to found a city. In the city you get trade and the specialized workers. In the surrounding lands are the densely farmed areas that supply the city with food.

Now you may ask "How do you know any of these things, Mr. Book Writer person? Were you there?" I learn mostly from the work of archeologists. They find hardened clay and stone items that do not biodegrade. They can look at stone carvings and pottery. Then they come up with ideas about what the bits of stone and pottery mean. It is not an exact science and agreement can be elusive. They find pottery bits in ruins all around the Fertile Crescent and figure out where it all came from. Stone buildings are durable, and they can find ruins of very old buildings indeed.

It should come as no surprise then, given how important water is for agriculture, that the first civilizations sprang up near major rivers. The earliest yet known was centered on the city of Uruk. This city, or the ruins of it today, can be found in the lower Tigris-Euphrates River valley. In the Bible, this region is known as the Plains of Shinar. Here in the late Fourth Millennium

(3500-3100 BC) there are plates, bowls and jars in a distinctive style that can be found as far away as Syria. There is also evidence of weaving, metalworking and stone cutting. The farms growing grain were augmented with date orchards. The nearby lands that were not suitable for growing crops were grazed by herdsmen that traded with the city. The river also provided for fishing and its marshes with hunting. Far more importantly for our purposes, by the end of this period there was the first known writing.

Now, secular archeologists see this identical material culture throughout the region, and they say that this means that the culture of Uruk was dominant. Uruk must have mass produced the pottery since people normally change things a little as they pass the technology around. Each city and town's pottery would be slightly different. This was not the case with the pottery of Uruk, which would require a level of mass production and distribution that was highly unusual in the ancient world.

There is an alternate explanation. If the people living in Uruk all suddenly left and moved all throughout the area, spreading all over the region, you would expect to see everyone using the same style for some time. The primary difficulty secular archeologists would have with this is that it corresponds to a narrative in Scripture. Now, I wasn't there, so I can't definitively say that this was the people spreading out after the episode of the tower of Babel. The Uruk site is referred to as Babel in some sources, along with a couple other locations. I would like to point out though that none of the archeologists were there either. Archeology is like that; different people have various interpretations of the evidence. All I am saying is that the timing, location, and material evidence is consistent with the Genesis narrative of the dispersal of man from a location on the plains of Shinar. In addition, this view is supported by written texts of great age that, were they not Scripture, would be considered important evidence to secular historians as well.

Something one gets used to when dealing with secular historians is a bit of a double standard. Written texts are normally used to help understand archeological discoveries. When it comes to Biblical texts, however, any tenable interpretation of the evidence that is different than that found in Scripture is preferred by the scholarly archeological community at large. The last thing academia wants today is to ever confirm Scripture. As a result, many of my interpretations of archeological finds will focus on the observations of the minority of archeologists who dare to point out the consistency of archeology with Scriptural accounts. This is because I come to this assuming the Scriptures to be authentic. You are less likely to find mainstream archeologists that will admit that their interpretation is based on their assumption of the opposite.

To understand how civilization came about, we need to talk about households. I have an entire section on this concept to help you understand ancient society with its very different structure than we typically see today. A quick summary for our purposes here: the household was how society was structured. It consisted of an extended family that cooperated to farm the land and produce goods and handicrafts. The household members also lived near each other and shared the goods they produced. It was like a really big family that always watched each other's backs. A wealthy household could also include workers who were not related to the family and who were paid in food and goods. The household also took care of those who could not work like the old and children. A city would have many households in it.

Initially, the largest and most wealthy "household" was the temple. It was the priest instead of the king that ruled most ancient cities. Each temple was a massive household. The largest and most ornate building in Uruk by far was the temple. All of the goods flowing in and out of the temple required the advent of a new sort of specialized laborer: the administrator. Unfortunately for their record keeping, paper and pencils had yet to be invented and their I-pad screens were cracked beyond usefulness. With their options so limited, these administrators made marks on clay tablets to keep record of the temple accounts. These marks would be the precursors to the first written language.

It is really interesting to see that the first governments were religious in nature. Today we believe that there should be a separation between church and state. We got that from an era of European history where governments would routinely persecute people of religions other than the one established by the government. Initially the role of gathering resources to distribute to the poor was done exclusively by religious organizations. Even today churches still do this but much of the safety net for the poor has become the job of the secular government instead. We have begun seeing city laws where people, even churches, are forbidden by law from feeding the homeless. It brings up some questions. To what extent has government become a religion?[3] Is total separation of church and state even possible? Can a government that fulfills the roles that religion has commonly filled exist without interfering decidedly in the free exercise of traditional religion?

Interestingly, writing from this long ago is easier to find than much of what is written much later. This is because it is written on clay tablets. Later people wrote on papyrus, woven reeds, and animal skins. These make better writing surfaces, but they rot away. Later clay writing can also be found so the progression from the early proto-cuneiform to the full-blown language can be seen.

---

3. Just think about it a bit. Totalitarian regimes want your heart, not just your obedience. Also, check out some churches around July 4th. Ouch.

The first symbols represented things like animals, quantities of grain and items of woven cloth called textiles. When people brought offerings to the gods, the administrators kept records of it. When the goods were distributed to the household or to those in need of aid, record was kept. The great thing about writing, as compared to other archeological finds, is that there is less guess work about what it means.

While Uruk was the oldest such city, the Fertile Crescent soon was filled with similar cities. They were heavily influenced by Uruk, were similar in how they were run and used the record keeping language. It is believed by some that as populations grew people moved off and founded new cities. During this time Uruk enjoyed cultural and political dominance. Others see in the end of Uruk God's judgment on men and see this dispersal as a sudden and dramatic abandonment of the site.

This brings us to government. Today we live in a world of territorial states. If you look at a map, there are well defined borders. The people who live in those countries are all part of the nation. Back in the ancient world I am telling you about, there are no such things. A city ruled over the people in the city and in the farmland around. The next city over, even if everyone there came from the first city, ran its own business. Cities might dominate other cities. They might make a neighboring city pay tribute or help them in war. Each city, though, had a measure of independence that modern cities would never dream of. There is no chance that Chicago might decide to form an alliance with New York and Los Angeles and sack Washington DC. Ancient cities always had that option if it should present itself.

This brings us to kings. You knew that there were not always kings. Who came up with the idea of having someone be king? It seems strangely unfair for one guy to be able to tell everyone else what to do. Somehow this sort of thing caught on to the extent that, for a while, you couldn't throw a stick without hitting one. It may come as a surprise to find out that it had nothing to do with strange women lying about in ponds distributing swords[4].

What happened was that conflict over control of agricultural lands between cities led to a greater frequency of armed conflict over them. These conflicts brought about the rise of mighty warriors who built up their households with lands and resources. In every area there are people who are more successful, whether it be through numbers, hard work or ruthlessness. They would also serve as protectors of the other households of the city in the case of conflict with another. These leaders built palaces that started to replace the temple as the most large and ornate building in the city. Government shifted from the temple to the king. At first these kings, or as they called them, lugals, started off as favorites who won their place by popular acclaim from fighting for the city. Soon, the lugals passed on their power to their children and cities had dynasties of kings.

The concept of king is important to understand since it is used as an image in the Bible with great frequency. At first glance it seems to be a pretty good thing to be king. The king has the authority in society and everyone else has to do what he says. Everything ultimately belongs to him, and he can demand anything in his realm, and it is given to him. He even gets to make up the rules everyone else has to live by. The job comes with considerable responsibility. By that I mean that just about everything is his responsibility. He is the one who protects the people from foreign threats who would harm them. He has to make sure that justice is done in every case. The innocent must be protected and the guilty must, without exception, be punished. Even making sure everyone is provided for is the responsibility of the king.

---

4. Much to the relief of Dennis in Monty Python and the Holy Grail.

Clearly, as long as the king does his job, having a king is a really good deal. The problem we have had as a species with kings, leading to us by and large chucking them, is that most kings do an awful job of it. Most kings do just fine with the "telling people what to do" and "making people give them things" departments. Where they mostly drop the ball is in the justice, provision, and protection end. For some reason they become so concerned with stoking their egos and crushing their opposition that making sure there is justice in the land sort of falls through the cracks. They somehow lose sight of their hungry subjects as making themselves fantastically wealthy takes priority. This sort of power seems to have the worst effect on people. As we move forward and witness the actions of rulers, see if you don't agree.

3

MESOPOTAMIA
3100 BC-1761 BC

Terah took Abram his son and Lot the son of Haran, his grandson, and Sarai his daughter-in-law, his son Abram's wife, and they went forth together from Ur of the Chaldeans to go into the land of Canaan, but when they came to Haran, they settled there.

By this time the world was no longer so much of a wilderness. It wasn't anywhere nearly as crowded as it is today but there were areas, particularly closer to the rivers, where people could be found in crowds. Further from the cities groups of men clad in skins or cloth could be seen standing guard over herds of sheep and goats. They set up their tents in small temporary villages, ready to move at a moment's notice. There were still vast uninhabited areas where animals were unfamiliar with man.

In and around the cities, new and exciting technologies were in use. Bronze tools aided in agriculture and other tasks. Pottery wheels produced fine vessels when used by the skilled craftsmen.

Bolts of cloth were made at looms, allowing for fine and comfortable, if expensive, clothing. Masons cut stones to make buildings that were both durable and well insulated. Trade caravans traveled long to get whatever things one couldn't find locally, from rare minerals and metals to crafts.

About 3100 BC, Uruk was destroyed. Information is sketchy, and we can only guess what happened. By this time, many other cities had grown to similar size. By the time it was rebuilt, the economic dominance of Uruk had come to a permanent end. Now there was a balance of power with many cities all over Mesopotamia. As we move into the Third Millennium BC in Mesopotamia, the cultural dominance of Uruk also faded. The culture, or way of doing things, in cities became more diverse. Each city had a temple to a different god. Sometimes there was more than one god, and each god had its own household in the city. The one that was the most powerful would be seen as ruling over the less powerful gods. Uruk was forced to share prominence with other Sumerian cities like Ur, Eridu, Umma and Lagash in southern Mesopotamia as well as Susa in Elam. By this time, it is clear that the Sumerians, the ethnicity that founded, or at least refounded, Uruk were not alone in the region.

To the east of southern Mesopotamia lay the Elamite city of Susa in modern day Iran. Its inhabitants had their own language and used the same cuneiform script as the people of southern Mesopotamia. The Elamites would serve as the foundation for the Persian culture and people. Far to the west, civilization rose along the Nile. Later we will talk about how this civilization unified quickly into something much more like our modern territorial state. We will need to treat it separately because of both its pivotal role in Scripture and the many issues involved in understanding it properly.

The Akkadians were a people who spoke a Semitic language

and had cities in the region to the north between and around the Tigris and Euphrates rivers. The Akkadians would come to dominate the southern part of Mesopotamia as well. Both Assyria and Babylon were Akkadian.

There were also herders who lived between the cities and functioned somewhat independently from the cities. These herders, Amorites, also spoke a Semitic language but were ethnically Canaanite[1]. According to archeology, these Amorites seem to have come from the west. Earliest records of them are from modern day Israel and Lebanon. They then moved east into modern day Syria, Jordan and Iraq. While they initially lived mostly in the lands between cities, herding on lands not suitable for growing grain, eventually some of them took over cities. If archeologists find Semitic names in the Near East in writings of this period that are not Akkadian, they will call them Amorite. Using their criteria, Abram would be considered an Amorite since he was Semitic, but not Akkadian. Obviously, Abram was descended from Shem, an entirely different son of Noah from Ham, the Amorites' ancestor. The Amorites also lived in areas further away from the rivers. Relations between the cities and the Amorites were not always peaceful.

It was after the fall of Uruk as "the city" in southern Mesopotamia that cuneiform writing was developed by Sumerian scribes. It is difficult to overemphasize how important this is for history. Now instead of getting notes on how many cows came into the temple on a given day, we can read letters or official accounts of battles. Rulers could document their wars and describe their reasons for going to war. We have lists of rulers. This writing is different from the writing you are likely used to. It is not alphabetical. Characters stand for syllables. It could be used to write in

---

1. Genesis 10: 15-16

other languages than Sumerian just as easily. It spread through the cities, and records can be found from all over the region. Based on these records we do have some idea of dynasties and rulers and the conflicts and politics that went on during the days of Abram, and even a bit before. This will allow us to look in this chapter at the history of Mesopotamia in the years just before and during the call of Abram from Ur and Haran.

While territorial states were not the normal thing in ancient Mesopotamia, this does not mean that empires did not form that controlled considerable areas. Control had to be extended city by city. Cities had ways of controlling each other given the opportunity. They could economically dominate them, making it a good a deal financially to obey the dominant power. They could be military allies gaining protection from the dominant city. Sometimes cities would attack and defeat another city. Most of the time the beaten city would agree to obey in return for protection. This arrangement is called a vassal suzerain treaty, and I have already explained what that is in the earlier section on Covenants. Occasionally, the victorious ruler would replace the loser with either a new, friendlier native ruler or occasionally appoint a governor from his own city over the beaten one.

Sargon of Akkad

Now we are going to look at a spot of ancient Mesopotamian political history. We will be moving over at fifty thousand feet at just shy of Mach 4. This is a Bible history book after all. There aren't all that many juicy details anyhow.

Power started to concentrate again in southern Mesopotamia when, about 2350 BC, after decades of being thrashed by the city of Lagash, the city of Umma finally got its revenge. A ruler named Lugal Zugesi took over Umma and then defeated and conquered

Ur and Uruk. He then turned his coalition of cities against Lagash and added it to his power base. All of these cities, you will notice, were close together below the narrow part between the rivers which will form the border between the regions of Assyria and Babylon later.

All good things come to an end; in this case the end for Lugal Zugesi came in the form of what is considered the first emperor, Sargon of Akkad. Sargon was initially the Lugal of Kish. He completed a sweep of Zugesi's subject cities, culminating in taking Uruk, where Lugal Zugesi had moved his capitol. Sargon then conquered south to the Persian Gulf, symbolically washing his weapons in the south sea. He established his rule by killing off Zugesi, having his own daughter appointed as high priestess of Inana in Ur and moving his capitol to Akkad. He now ruled Southern Mesopotamia. He was able to extend his influence through Syria to the Mediterranean with trade. His Akkadian Empire raided into Elam regularly, causing the dynasty there to move east from Susa to avoid his attentions.

Controlling so much territory gave early empires access to lots of valuable things. First they could get metals, particularly copper and tin to make bronze, the metal of choice for weapons at the time. They were also able to get luxury goods and exotic merchandise like spices and strange animals. All of these things went to enhance the prestige of the Lugal. Control of so much area also allowed wealth from trade as people had to pay to use the roads on their trade routes.

Sargon's death in 2280 BC was not the end of his empire. It did mean that the other cities would try to assert their independence. People were not yet used to having to obey distant rulers. City rulers wanted their autonomy. His sons fought against frequent rebellions and had to deal with revenge raids from Elam. The empire actually expanded under his grandson Naram Sin. Naram

Sin conquered Susa and placed a governor over it. He also militarily subjugated Ebla and Mari in Syria.

It was a good run but after Naram Sin died, about 2218 BC, the empire fell. In addition to the frequent rebellions, barbarians called Gutians, from the Zagros Mountains in modern day Iran, overran the heartland of the empire. Soon the rulers of the cities were replaced by Gutian conquerors. Given his age, Abram would have been born under their rule. The Gutians were expelled by native Sumerians who set up a brief dynasty called Ur III, but this too fell to drought, rebellion and the arrival of a type of barbarian called the Amorite. It is during Ur III that Abram was called along with his father's household from Ur to Haran. Haran is in Syria, much further north and far closer to Canaan.

Between the Ur III empire's fall and the rise of the first Assyrian empire, all of the events in Genesis from Abraham to Joseph will take place. What follows in this section is what was going on in Mesopotamia while Israel was in Egypt.

Hammurabi

The next Empire would be set up from the northern part of Mesopotamia in what will come to be known as Assyria. Two powerful cities were slugging it out. Mari, led by Yahdun-Lim went back and forth with Esh Nunna under Shamshi Adad. Shamshi Adad came out on top and used the power gained from his victory to found the first Assyrian Empire. It didn't last long but it set the stage for future Assyrian Empires. In this case, Shamshi Adad's puppet ruler in Esh Nunna was overthrown and the new ruler fought against him instead. Aleppo in Syria was also powerful and struck Shamshi Adad from the other side. Together they were too much. He was unable to recover and lost both his empire and his life.

Before he kicked off, Shamshi Adad had worked with the leader of Babylon, a guy known as Hammurabi. Hammurabi's family had taken over Babylon earlier in 1880 BC and had spread out a bit from there. Hammurabi ascended the throne in 1792 BC. While dominant over a few local cities, Hammurabi was not a major power. Evidence is that he accepted protection from Shamshi Adad initially and concentrated his efforts on improving the irrigation works in Babylon, winning over important people from neighboring cities with generous gifts and improving the walls around the cities loyal to him.

Mari, which Shamshi Adad had conquered, rose back up after Adad's death and took over the majority of Shamshi Adad's cities to dominate the northern area of Mesopotamia. Mari soon made an alliance with Elam and together they conquered Esh Nunna. The Elamites were a separate group from the east of Mesopotamia. If you recall, they got pushed around pretty good by Sargon's empire and had been getting their own back by pushing the Sumerians in Ur around to no small extent. They ended up putting a puppet of their own choosing over Esh Nunna after it was taken. Elam followed up the gains by launching raids against Babylon and Larsa, the other southern Mesopotamian power.

Larsa was no lightweight. In fact, had you wanted to take bets on who would come out as the dominant Mesopotamian power in all of this, you would have done well to drop your whole bankroll on Larsa. It controlled the chief religious city of Nippur along with Ur, Uruk, Isin, Umma and Lagash. Elam also was aware of Larsa's power and concentrated its attacks against it.

Elam decided to facilitate its attacks on Babylon and Larsa with a spot of trickery. The Elamites sent word to each that they were commanded to send troops to aid Elam in the conquest of the other. They fooled precisely nobody, and the result was an alliance between Larsa and Babylon focused on ending Elam's reign of terror.

Elam, for its part, moved its reign of terror north by launching sieges on cities controlled by its previous ally, Mari. Hammurabi led Babylon along with Mari and Esh Nunna against the Elamites. He broke the sieges of allied cities and launched a series of costly raids on Elamite lands; costly, that is, for the Elamites. Now if you were paying attention, you might have noticed that Esh Nunna was supposed to be on Elam's side as a puppet. Its changing sides was both a blow to Elam and evidence of Hammurabi's diplomatic skill in getting it to switch sides. Elam was badly damaged, its evil schemes nipped in the bud. Hammurabi was covered in a visible aura of glory.

Did you notice that Larsa did not participate in the battles, despite being allied with Babylon for the expressed purpose of fighting Elam? Hammurabi sure did. The next war season, he laid siege to Larsa itself. He took the city and broke down the walls. He did not, however, burn it down. He established his rule over Larsa and its satellite cities. With Babylon and Larsa's considerable power at his back, Hammurabi was able to take Esh Nunna the next year and follow it up with the conquest of Mari the year after. By 1761 BC Hammurabi had established his empire by conquering all of Mesopotamia. The Old Babylonian Empire was formed, and Babylon would be a city of incredible power and influence for the next one thousand five hundred years.

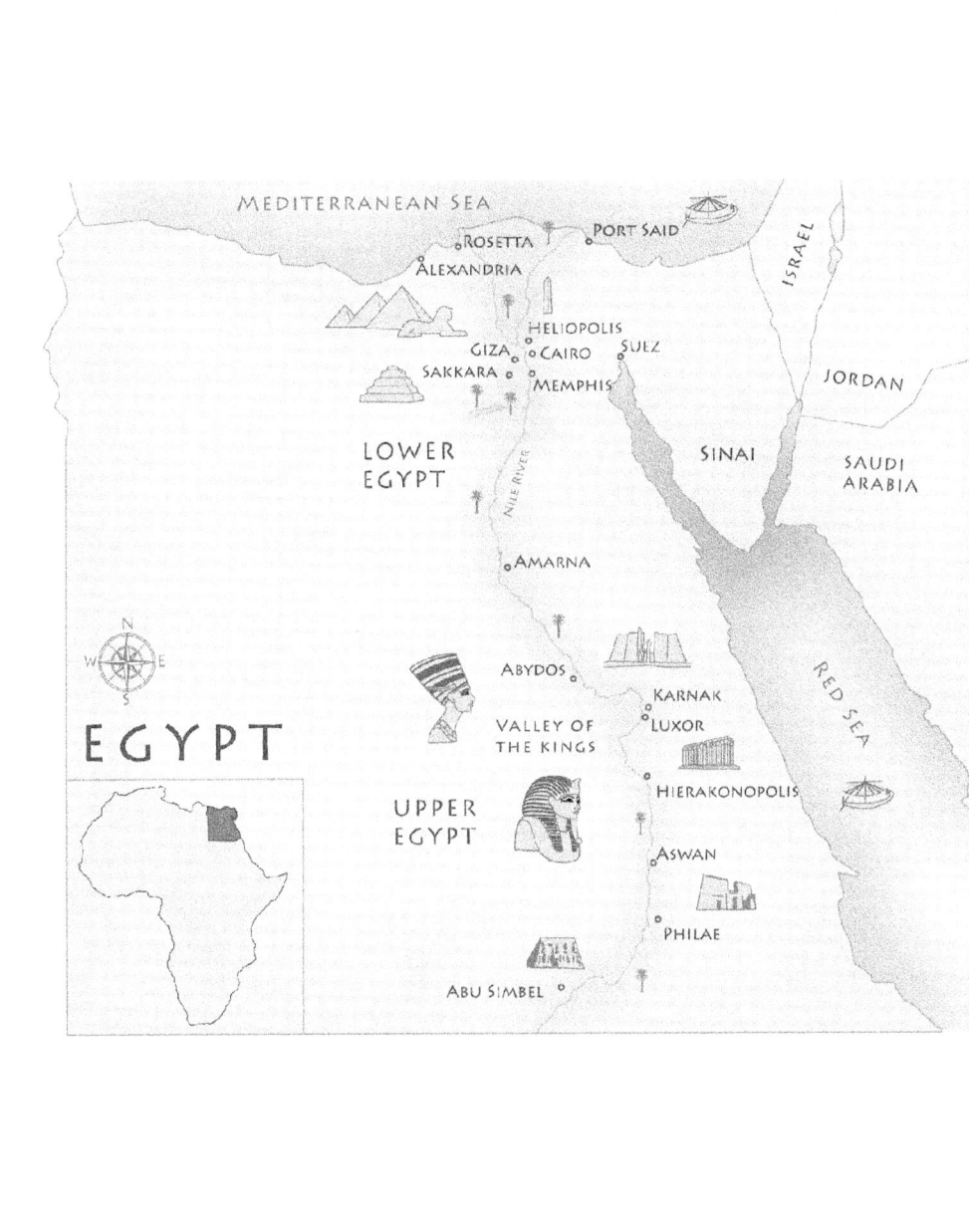

4

ANCIENT EGYPT

> *Now when they had departed, behold, an angel of the Lord appeared to Joseph in a dream and said, "Rise, take the child and his mother, and flee to Egypt, and remain there until I tell you, for Herod is about to search for the child, to destroy him." And he rose and took the child and his mother by night and departed to Egypt and remained there until the death of Herod. This was to fulfill what the Lord had spoken by the prophet, "Out of Egypt I called my son."*

Meanwhile in northeastern Africa, Egypt was forming. While Mesopotamia had two rivers and occasional massive flooding, Egypt had one river with regular annual flooding. You would think that would be a bad thing, but in fact it was incredibly good. The key idea is "regular." The flooding deposited fertile silt all over the agricultural land around it and then receded in time for planting. In order to understand Egypt, you have to understand the Nile. The Nile flows from south to north. Going down the Nile means going north and similarly going up the Nile means going south. The kingdom of Upper Egypt is south of the kingdom of Lower Egypt. You get the picture. The waters that feed into the Nile from the Ethiopian highlands increase drastically when the rainy season hits Ethiopia, causing those regular floods. The waters that do not come from those highlands are steadier year-round, so the Nile does not dry up.

The second important feature of Egypt is the desert. Other than the Nile River valley, Egypt is mostly desert. This includes the granddaddy of all the "get lost among the sand dunes and die of thirst" deserts, the Sahara[1]. This means that the civilization in Egypt lies along the Nile. Another fascinating feature of this combination of Nile and desert is how it connects two worlds. The Sahara Desert forms an effective barrier between the worlds north and south of it. Contact between Asia and northern Africa with Africa below the Sahara is extremely limited for much of history. The Egyptians could follow the Nile south to Nubia and Kush. For a very long time, Europe and Asia had access to the goods and culture of sub-Saharan Africa almost exclusively through Egypt.

Together, the Nile and desert created an environment where the people of Egypt could live in relative safety and isolation from much of the rest of the world. In addition to hunting and fishing in the fertile region, Egyptians imported emmer wheat and barley from Mesopotamia and agriculture flourished to no small extent. In this environment two kingdoms formed from farming and fishing communities. Lower Egypt lay next to the Mediterranean

---

1. There is a theory that the Sahara was more humid and less deserty initially and the people who settled along the Nile were able for some time to live further from it but concentrated as the Sahara dried out.

while Upper Egypt was further south along the Nile. At some point these two kingdoms combined to form a united kingdom[2].

In most cases, the difficulty that would cause us to be unsure of exactly what happened would be because nobody wrote anything down. In Egypt we have a very different problem. The reason we have a hard time being sure of exactly what happened is because we have too much written down. Much of what we have is from tombs of kings and high officials. The crux of the difficulty is that these Pharaohs liked to claim accomplishments that were not, strictly speaking, their own. I had grown up being taught that Menes or Narmer united Egypt but now these claims are drowned out in a storm of conflicting information. There is now evidence of the existence of an earlier Pharaoh, Scorpion, wearing the crown of Upper and Lower Egypt. Narmer still may be the one who united the crowns, but it is now impossible to say with certainty.

Dates can also be tricky when dealing with Ancient Egypt. We have king lists, again multiple sources, that do not agree. Some are missing Pharaohs; others list dynasties that were ruling different parts of Egypt simultaneously as if they occurred one after the other. Pharaoh was supposed to be the incarnation of a god and having more than one at the same time did not work with their religious beliefs. As a result, it is difficult to say definitively what was happening until we can hook up the events with the far more reliable Assyrian chronology. As a result, dates in Ancient Egypt are approximate.

With those things in mind, we can say that unification in Egypt came about roughly 3000 BC. After this, we begin with the dynasties of the Old Kingdom, even though we do know of previous Predynastic Pharaohs, who ruled prior to the so called First

---

2. Forming the basis of the claims of the British Museum to the pyramids once they could find a way to pick them up and move them to London.

Dynasty. These Predynastic Pharaohs had tombs, and in those tombs we find objects of wealth like gold, silver, precious stones, and perfumes. They also had the bodies of servants, entertainers, dogs, and lions. These extra bodies were no doubt very much alive when they entered the tomb. They remained in the tomb to provide service to their king after it was sealed. Fortunately, this practice did not last long.

The writing, called Hieroglyphics, was pictographic; it looked like the objects it represented. This writing was found in tombs and on stone monuments called stele. Writings could also be found on pottery, like the sort in Mesopotamia. Egyptians also wrote on papyrus, but Old Kingdom was a long time ago and papyrus degrades eventually, even in a dry place like Egypt.

It is in tombs that most of our written information of the Old Kingdom is found. It is fortunate indeed then that the Old Kingdom is famous for its tomb building. The Third through Fifth Dynasties produced the oldest and most massive tombs known to man. Many of them are still standing to this day.

This raises the question: What is up with those Egyptians and tombs? Naturally it is about burying the dead and their religious beliefs about the afterlife. Initially, Egyptians would bury their dead in the sands of the desert. Unfortunately, jackals would dig up their dearly departed and gnaw on them to an extent. Spending the hereafter in a scavenger's digestive tract was not the afterlife most Egyptians were aiming for. Those who could afford to do so began placing dried mud bricks on top of the graves so the scavengers could not get to them. Obviously if commoners can have bricks on their graves, the Pharaoh should have something far fancier. It quickly got out of hand as Pharaohs demonstrated their magnificence by building ever more elaborate tombs.

Old Kingdom Egypt

They had this magnificence because Egypt was a highly centralized state. That means that during much of the Old Kingdom regional officials had little power and the rules of society were handed down from the capitol. There is evidence of a highly developed bureaucracy. At the center of control and power, Pharaoh ruled with unlimited authority. Because of this power and control, the Pharaohs of the Old Kingdom could call for and organize massive building projects.

As I go over some of these building projects, I want you to notice how intelligent the Egyptians must have been to show such high levels of logistics, government, planning, engineering and architecture. They show precisely the same sort of intelligence as modern men. Five thousand years further from the fictional simian ancestor and we do not seem superior in our abilities as the evolutionist's myth would call for.

The great builders of the Old Kingdom were, as I mentioned, in the Third to Fifth Dynasties. They ruled between 2700 and 2350 BC roughly. Their capitols were near Cairo and Memphis. The big breakthrough happened under Djoser. He had a vizier named Imhotep who made for Djoser a burial monument or Mastaba out of stone instead of dried mud brick. Now a Mastaba is just a big flat slab that goes over the tomb. Imhotep then added four more slabs on top of the first, each slightly smaller than the last, forming a step pyramid. So, you could say that this Imhotep invented pyramids.

Towards the beginning of the Fourth Dynasty a Pharaoh named Sneferu built three, count them, three pyramids. The first was a step pyramid that he then tried to encase in smoother stones. The stones fell off, making a heap of rubble. His second attempt was a true pyramid, but the angle was too steep. The builders changed the angle in the middle of construction with the result being a curved pyramid. His last attempt was a successful pyramid at the angle of the top of his second one. Because of the color of the rock, this one is called the Red Pyramid. So, you could say that Sneferu invented "third time is the charm."

Sneferu's successor was Pharaoh Khufu. His pyramid was the largest one ever made and the only wonder of the ancient world still standing. It is made of over two million blocks with an average weight of almost three tons each. Scholars still argue about how the ancient Egyptians were able to transport and lay with precision blocks that sometimes weighed fourteen tons and did not need mortar since they were carved straight. What scholars do not argue about so much is if it was built by slaves[3]. Consensus these days is that it was done by professional builders. The idea that the Hebrew slaves built these pyramids has never been seriously considered, except on weak television documentaries[4]. They were built far too early.

Khufu's son Khafra built a pyramid next to his father's. It was slightly smaller. The reason it was close to his father's pyramid was so that they could be part of the same funerary complex. Today they can still be seen side by side near Cairo. After Khafra, the pyramids became smaller, and gradually new sorts of tombs that did not require most of a nation's resources to build came into fashion among the Pharaohs.

What is a funerary complex? I am so glad you asked. You see, these massive tombs for the Pharaohs were all about providing the best afterlife possible for them once they departed. These complexes around the tombs were so that priests could live on site

---

3. Aliens, maybe, but slaves, no.
4. The same sort that will tell you they found the tomb of Jesus but refrain from mentioning this particular Jesus was from the second century and just had the same name.

to perform their duties. The idea was to have these sites be staffed with priests venerating the Pharaoh perpetually. Unfortunately, this never did work out as they would be abandoned eventually, particularly once the dynasty of said Pharaoh was over.

The funny part about changing dynasties was that Egyptians saw a danger in annoying the spirits of the old Pharaohs by abandoning them. What they would do was knock the noses off of their statues. The statue was supposed to hold the Ka of the Pharaoh it depicted. Knocking off the nose kept the statue and the Ka it contained from breathing. This was supposed to hinder any supernatural vengeance. This vengeance avoidance hack could also be used by tomb robbers.

In addition to building fancy tombs, the Old Kingdom had miners in Sinai to bring back mineral wealth. Just before Djoser, we have record of his brother, Nebka, sending expeditions to Sinai to mine both copper and turquoise. They also had access to large amounts of gold from Upper Egypt. What they did not have, and badly needed to trade for, were usable lumber, and tin to make bronze. They had trade with Byblos and were always looking for ways to control the east coast of the Mediterranean. Trade went south along the Nile as well. There were military ventures against tribes in Libya and Nubia, bringing them into subjugation. As a result, as time went by Egypt's population and culture were influenced by their northern Levantine, and sub-Saharan African neighbors.

Middle Kingdom Egypt

About 2300 BC, the power of the Pharaohs began to wane, and the power of local officials began to grow at their expense. A region of Egypt was called a Nome. The Nomarchs, or governors, began handing down their titles to their sons. Fancy tombs with magic spells to aid in the afterlife began to appear for non-Pharaohs as well. As local lords increased their power, the reach of Pharaoh shortened. Nubia broke free and became independent. The Egyptian control of Sinai became weak. Libyans raided Egyptian settlements. The weak pharaohs of the Ninth and Tenth Dynasties moved their capitol to Herakleopolis by the Delta in Lower Egypt while a rival Eleventh Dynasty set up at Thebes in Upper Egypt. This time of regional strife and lack of central control is known as the First Intermediary Period.

The First Intermediary Period came to an end after Mentuhotep II of the Eleventh Dynasty overcame the weaker northern kingdom and once again united the two crowns of Egypt. This marked the beginning of the Middle Kingdom. It is into the Middle Kingdom that Abram will come with his wife/sister Sarai.

5

THE PATRIARCHS AND ANCIENT WARFARE

Then one who had escaped came and told Abram the Hebrew, who was living by the oaks of Mamre the Amorite, brother of Eshcol and of Aner. These were allies of Abram. When Abram heard that his kinsman had been taken captive, he led forth his trained men, born in his house, 318 of them, and went in pursuit as far as Dan. And he divided his forces against them by night, he and his servants, and defeated them and pursued them to Hobah, north of Damascus. Then he brought back all the possessions, and also brought back his kinsman Lot with his possessions, and the women and the people.

Night had fallen several hours before and in the camp below the campfires had begun to burn low. The invaders made no effort to hide their camp and posted few guards. After all, they had laid the bodies of their enemies on the ground. They believed that there could be no pursuit. In their imagination, there were none left to pursue them. They believed they had gotten away with it so now dwelled in safety. The invaders had miscalculated badly. The Chieftain had tracked them for one hundred fifty miles with a single purpose, and tonight they would meet their end. The Chieftain signaled to his allies, who moved to approach the camp from the other side. He began moving silently towards the unsuspecting soldiers. His men, a little over three hundred strong, followed closely after, hefting their spears. The Chieftain's men would come upon the invaders in their blankets. There would be few survivors.

The scene above might seem like something from a story of legendary warriors like American Indians tracking their enemies on a raid. In fact, this is an event from the fourteenth chapter of Genesis. The Chieftain was Abram. This is a Bible story you probably never heard in Sunday school. At least you probably never thought of it like this. In this chapter, I will use this passage as a springboard into various matters in the ancient world.

Raiding was a common part of almost every culture where there was not a great centralized power. Taking what belongs to others is easier than growing or making it yourself. Men will, if they think they can get away with it, routinely turn bandit. Now, it is better to rob people who do not know who you are or where you live, or they might get help, revenge and their stuff back, in that order. It makes sense to travel to nearby people not of your group to do your bit of smash and grab. This sort of thing is in the background of endless disputes and why neighboring peoples often break out into violence with each other. Even if the wise, level headed older men want to keep the peace, the younger guys can be hard to control. What is more, kings and nobles are not immune to the temptation and can turn to raiding just as quickly as young men. In fact, much warfare in the ancient world was of this sort instead of for the purpose of conquest.

During the age of the Patriarchs, cities ruled over themselves for the most part. Sometimes more powerful cities would make deals with smaller, weaker ones. These deals were called treaties or covenants. Larger cities would agree not to attack and destroy the weaker cities and to protect them from attack by other cities. The weaker cities in return would pay tribute to the stronger cities and agree to send soldiers to help them when they went to war. These were called vassal suzerain treaties. The weaker city was the vassal. The stronger one was the suzerain[1].

I bring this up because such an arrangement had been in effect in Canaan as we began the narrative of Genesis chapter fourteen. Specifically, we learn that Sodom and Gomorrah and some of their allies had decided to try their luck by breaking their treaty and refusing to send tribute to their former suzerain, Elam. Chedorlaomer king of Elam, a city in modern day Iran, gathered his vassals and traveled to punish Sodom and Gomorrah with a military raid. Before he went against them, Chedorlaomer raided the surrounding region as well. The raid was very successful. The Elamite coalition defeated the rebels and sacked their cities. They took items of value, livestock, and slaves, from both the rebels and the other cities. After returning, the normal course would be for the defeated kings, or their successors if they had died, to sue for peace and agree to a new treaty. Up to this point, things had gone as well as could be hoped.

In this instance, Chedorlaomer had not counted on taking captive the nephew of one of the local chiefs from the surrounding countryside. At this time, the countryside around the cultivated

---

1. You already know this if you have read the section on covenants but I am loath to leave anybody behind.

areas in the Fertile Crescent contained groups of herders that could be quite formidable. Abram was such a chief. The Bible said he had over three hundred men fit for war in his service. He was also allied with Amorite chieftains who had men fit for war as well.

Abram's men were not specialized soldiers. Instead, they filled a number of roles. First, they did watch the herds and guide them in grazing. They also served to protect the flock from predators. They were, after all, primarily shepherds. Lastly, the massive herds Abram owned were very valuable, and his men had to be able to protect them from raiders. There were no police to call if thieves came to poach his herds. The protection of the life and property of Abram and his household was ultimately his responsibility. To further protect his herds, Abram was allied with the Amorites who lived in the area. Anyone who wanted to steal from a herder in Canaan would have to deal with a large, dangerous coalition. Not reckoning on having to contend with this coalition would prove very costly indeed for Chedorlaomer and his vassals.

In ancient society, having a large army of men who did nothing but train and go to war was rare. In the section on agriculture, we learned that most people had to work to produce food. Civilizations near rivers often had the largest professional armies but even so they were not particularly large in comparison to the population. Herder or farmer groups in Canaan would have little more than personal guards for their king.

Imagine living in a place where there were no police. No state or national military existed to protect you. You would need to take care of your own property. What we would call civilians had to take up weapons and defend themselves. Professional warfare is a much more recent innovation. In ancient times, farmers and herders were often warriors as well at need.

This was necessary since raiding was so common. In a world

where there were often not strong national governments, many people lived their whole lives raiding others. Raiding was also, as we can see from the account in Genesis, a normal tactic in war. Today crossing into enemy territory, robbing a couple communities, enslaving some of the people and then returning would be looked down on in the international community. Back then it was a normal part of life. This is why the Israelites in I Samuel asked Samuel for a king like the nations around them. They desired to be protected from their enemies.

The king would be the head of a powerful house that was able to protect the other people in the community. Often kings ruled no more than a city and the surrounding agricultural lands. A chieftain, like Abram, could be comparable in power to a king militarily. While such chieftains did not normally have as much population, and thus number of men, or the safety of city walls for shelter, they had the advantage of being mobile.

Mobility is an important thing in ancient society. It makes it difficult to strike a population that moves around. The Comanche bands of the southern American Great Plains were nomadic, and it gave them an advantage over both the Apache, who were semi nomadic when they contested the Great Plains and even the US which was an industrial civilization. You can plan ambush strikes to raid stationary foes and escape. If they cannot find you, or if they at least cannot find you safely, you can raid more or less with impunity.

Those who raise cereal crops do not have this luxury. They need to stay with their village. Defending them required either sending military expeditions against the enemy, the old "do unto others before they can do unto you" or, in the case of a large enemy force, the safety of city walls. Herders in ancient Palestine were in no way as mobile or difficult to track as the horse mounted American Indians. Herders still had to drive large groups of animals to move around. That meant that gathering an army to attack them was a feasible move.

Now, cities back then were much smaller than they are today. Most people lived outside the cities. The cities, though, were often surrounded with walls. The safety of walls in Canaan was often times supplemented by building them on mountains or hills. A fortress on top of a sheer cliff or a massive rock could offer incredible safety. Getting to such a secure location could mean survival against even overwhelming enemy armies. The great Assyrian Empire was able to take almost all of Judah after seizing all of Israel, but the walls of Jerusalem withstood it. Even the Roman Empire, master in its time of siegecraft, had a difficult time taking Jerusalem, and even more so conquering the fortress of Masada.

In the Bible, God is often referred to as a rock. It helps to understand that in that time, a rock was the foundation for safety in even the most dangerous situations. Understanding the importance of having a strong king who can defeat your enemies for daily safety will help you understand the imagery in the Bible where the Messiah is presented as a great king.

From the site of the Elamite victory over Sodom and Gomorrah in the region of the Dead Sea to where Abram's coalition ambushed them, near Dan, was about one hundred fifty miles. They would not go east. East would be across desert. Instead, they would head northeast across the fertile lands. Once to modern day Syria, they would head south along the roads of Mesopotamia. This route was longer but there would be water. This was why they went north to Dan. The Biblical record states that Abram divided his forces against them at night. This indicates that Abram and his allies ambushed the Elamites, likely because it would nullify their greater numbers.

Ambush at night was a very effective tactic in the ancient world. Sleeping opponents do not fight back and cannot dodge a spear thrust. Those awakened would be unarmored and disoriented. A well-executed ambush would force enemies to flee for their lives, leaving behind weapons and armor. If the camp did not have time to assemble its warriors into formation, each man would have to choose between flight and facing a group of enemy warriors. Such fights would be one sided. One man fighting a group generally only goes well for the one in action movies. Abram's ambush seemed to come off without a hitch since the Bible says he and his men chased the fleeing Elamites north of Damascus. The Elamite party must have been massive. The number of pitched battles they won showed their military effectiveness. Crushing such a powerful enemy, even given the ambush, shows the hand of God supporting Abram and fighting for him.

In the ancient world most warriors did not die in the battle itself. Most died in the rout once one side's formation broke. Fleeing soldiers would drop weapons and shields and run to escape victorious enemies who chased them. Twenty to thirty miles was a very good day's travel on foot. That is if the terrain is flat and clear. Here we find that the Elamites fled for about fifty miles before Abram's crew gave up the chase. That is a long time to run for your life.

After the slaughter of the Elamites, Abram returned with the captives and loot recovered from the raid. He had rescued his nephew Lot along with his household. The Bible then details the interactions of Abram, covered in glory from crushing the mighty coalition with the kings of Sodom and Salem.

Western Asia in the time of the Patriarchs

Canaan, during the time of Abraham, was populated by cities that ruled their surrounding villages and farms. These city kings, in turn, were mostly vassals of the Pharaoh in Egypt. They ran their own business but were bound by covenants. These city dwellers, we learn from Scripture, were filled with immorality, idolatry, and wickedness. Not least of the wickedness was the prevalence of child sacrifice. At this point in time, God was showing patience until the time of judgment. This judgment would come through the arrival of Abraham's descendants.

In between the cities, there were powerful herders like Abraham and his Amorite allies. Herders like Abraham moved around a fair bit to find food for their flocks. This is why the Patriarchs seem to be traveling almost constantly, visiting kings, and telling half truths about their relationships[2].

In the Second Millennium BC, the societal elites in the cities made heavy demands on the local peasants in the surrounding villages in Syria and Palestine which caused peasants to go into debt and slavery. The peasants fled their overlords in the cities to live in the countryside as outcasts and outlaws. These people are mentioned in the Amarna letters as Habiru. The fact that Habiru and Hebrew sound alike and both Habiru and the patriarchs lived in the areas in between cities as herders causes some to see the Habiru as ancestors of Israel.

While Hebrews may sound similar to Habiru, they were not the same. Habiru has entomology in Akkadian meaning "robber" or "displaced" and in Sumerian meaning "murder." Hebrew is derived from Heber, an ancestor of Abraham. While both groups were rural pastoralists, the Hebrews were not murderers and robbers, at least not any more than most. While Habiru were in the area for a long time and changed sides in the wars in Canaan, the Hebrews were consistently hostile to the Canaanites after they appeared. This is not to say that they could not be confused for

---

2. I'm looking at you, Abram and Isaac.

one another. One invading herder might look much like another to a city dweller watching them come over the walls.

The history given in Genesis is provided by Moses for the purpose of informing the returning Israelites of things they would need to know when they got to the Promised Land. Not every people group in the region would be Canaanites who needed to be eradicated. The story of Canaan being cursed for the sin of Ham draws a distinction between those who are living in the area and the people who are to be eradicated as the Israelites enter the land.

The Moabites and Ammonites were descended from Lot, Abram's nephew. While the children of Israel would later quarrel violently with both of them, they were their relatives, not Canaanites destined for destruction.

The Edomites were even more closely related since they were descendants of Abram and Isaac but not of Jacob. Of all of the people groups to be found in the region, the Edomites were the most closely related to Israel. While the Israelites were multiplying in Egypt, the Edomites were settling into the desert regions south of the Dead Sea. While they too fought from time to time, it is clear they were to be looked on as brothers. Their close relation sets the stage for those accusations of betrayal in Obadiah.

Perhaps a bit less obviously, we see that Abram lived in Haran in Syria and so did Laban, who was related to him. Jacob's wives were both from Laban's house as well. From this we see that there is a certain kinship between the Israelites and at least some of the people living in Syria. Abraham also had a child by an Egyptian and several sons from his second marriage, after Sarah died, by a woman called Keturah. From their children, we get Arabs, Ishmaelites and Midianites.

Now this might really blow your mind. The Philistines were not Canaanites either in the sense of being descended from

Canaan. While to all appearances in lifestyle and religion they were indistinguishable from the Canaanites, they were descended from Canaan's brother, Egypt or Mizraim[3]. Abraham and Isaac encountered them primarily in the role of rulers of cities which they drew near while they were herding. The nomadic patriarchs dug wells for their herds, and the Philistines seized them and plugged them back up. This would concern us far less except they would play an important part once the descendants of Jacob returned to the land.

---

3. Genesis 10:13-14

6

WHO WROTE GENESIS – DEUTERONOMY?

> *Anyone who has set aside the law of Moses dies without mercy on the evidence of two or three witnesses. How much worse punishment, do you think, will be deserved by the one who has trampled underfoot the Son of God?*

We all grew up hearing that the answer is Moses, but is it true? Secular historians assign the authorship to people who lived many hundreds of years later. Dates for the writing are given from the Tenth through Sixth Centuries BC. That is five to nine hundred years after Moses! These late dates are given to avoid any problems with fulfilled prophecy and divine foreknowledge that would conflict with their naturalistic worldview and to rob the text of the authority of Mosaic, and ultimately divine, authorship. Instead, they would have the account be a forgery in the name of Moses in order to advance the pernicious quest for spiritual power of priests in Jerusalem. Because of this, these claims represent slander against the honesty of God and the trustworthiness of His revelation and must be answered.

The primary difficulty for the idea that some priest, instead of Moses, wrote the Pentateuch is that the Biblical account is full of details that are now known to be accurate for the times they purport to come from. The Hebrews made bricks from mud and straw, instead of without straw, as was done in Israel in the time the critics claim the Pentateuch was written. The customs of the patriarchs depicted in Genesis are consistent with practices in that part of the world during the Twentieth Century BC. It is pretty incredible that an author from the Sixth Century would know of these practices. The idea of Sixth Century priests knowing of them stretches credulity. Place names have been discovered by Egyptologists that had been lost. Those same place names were alleged to be fabrications within the Scriptural narrative before they were discovered again. These are all details that, while they do not prove the narrative, do show knowledge of the realities of the time. These realities were not at all likely to be known five hundred to a thousand years later.

Even more telling is the form the law was given in. The law as given to Moses is in a form strikingly similar to the vassal suzerain covenants of the Fifteenth Century BC, which follow the Hittite style. This style was not followed six hundred to a thousand years later, and there is no reason to believe that Tenth through Sixth Century redactors had any access or knowledge of treaties in this style unless you count the law itself [1]. Even more telling is that the second giving of the law in Deuteronomy is even more strikingly similar to this Hittite model. The treaty style that a Sixth Century priest would be familiar with would be the Assyrian covenant,

---

1. Which you can't if your contention is that they wrote it later. That would be a paradox.

which lacks some of the elements of the Hittite. Deuteronomy has elements which point out that the final form of the document must have been written by someone who was familiar with the Hittite form. This is because the form and style are not things you pull from sources but products of the final authorship.

In order to explain this, critics create an elaborate system of sources that the supposed redactor[2] used to write his account. This allows the narrative to have authentic details yet still be a forgery that can be regarded with skepticism. The question that is raised is, if they have authentic sources from earlier ages, why do they obfuscate them behind what would at the time have been an obvious pretense ? If someone today were to claim to have found something written by a famous figure from a thousand years in the past, such as William the Conqueror, they would be able to expect only the greatest of skepticism. If they had legitimate sources, as the situation would require, they could much more easily gain credibility for their religious hoax with the names of the authentic sources attached. However, if Moses was not an authentic figure in the history of Israel, well known to the people, why would anyone care if he was the author? If Moses was an authentic historical figure, what was he famous for, if not receiving the law and writing it down for the people? If Moses was the author of one or more of the sources, what forgery could replace his authentic writing?

A further difficulty with this argument boils down to the need for centuries of Israelite clerics who all conspired to continually replace true accounts from authentic sources with inventions and lies. Furthermore, they were able to somehow do so without making any noticeable errors in historical customs or creating any

---

2. Someone who uses an earlier writing as a source for his new or heavily edited writing.

anachronisms. It is relatively easy to spot inventions of this sort. Take for example the book of Mormon, which has numerous anachronisms and errors involving time, place and culture. Metal weapons are said to be used in the Americas and horses ridden[3]. Jesus appeared and made illustrations to the Meso-Americans that would only make sense if they had been under Roman rule. Geography was described that does not exist in the Americas or anywhere else in the world. Israelites crafted oceangoing vessels and crossed oceans that the most seafaring people of their day did not even dare to enter. In Scripture we learn that whenever Israel needed to cross so much as a river, God had to dry it up for them. Joseph Smith had better access to historical accounts than Tenth through Sixth Century BC redactors, yet you can find such errors by the score in his alterations of Scriptural narrative. Critics of the Bible have yet to find one. They point to lack of specific confirmation and lack of current knowledge of places and peoples mentioned therein. That is why it is such a blow to their arguments every time a detail from the clouded past is found that confirms even the plausibility of the Scriptural narrative.

So, who wrote Genesis through Deuteronomy? Mostly Moses. Someone else needed to write chapter thirty-four of Deuteronomy which records the death and burial of Moses. This part of the text seems to be a postscript to the rest of the work. The text is still divinely inspired as God breathed out his revelation to the man or men who wrote this postscript. While many look to Joshua for this writing I believe it was another. I think it would need to be one of the last prophets of Israel prior to the silence in revelation that divided the Old Testament from the New.

The reason why is drawn from the text. The writer here states

---

3. There was some bronze working in South and Central America later but they had to wait for Spain for horses.

that God buried Moses after his death, and nobody knows where that is to this day.[4] This would hardly be noteworthy if Joshua were writing this. The man was already old when Moses died. The other reason is that Moses instructed the children of Israel that God would raise up a prophet like him from among them[5]. They needed to heed that prophet. Yet in verse ten it states that there had never arisen a prophet like Moses. This sounds like something one would say after seeing a great many prophets, not some time before the next one arose. No, this sounds like a summary statement on the Old Testament Era. The one who God would raise up, the one that Moses ordered them to heed, was still to come. Israel was still awaiting Him as Divine silence engulfed them.

---

4. Deuteronomy 34:6
5. Deuteronomy 18:15

7

EGYPT: THE SOJOURN YEARS

Then Pharaoh sent and called Joseph, and they quickly brought him out of the pit. And when he had shaved himself and changed his clothes, he came in before Pharaoh.

The Twelfth Dynasty of Pharaohs ruled Egypt when Jacob and his sons arrived in 1876 BC. This was the last stable dynasty of the Middle Kingdom period. The Thirteenth somehow lost control of Lower, or northern, Egypt. It seems there were too many people from the Near East moving in there[1]. As a result, the Thirteenth Dynasty moved its capitol south to Thebes and left the north to the newcomers.

While the Thirteenth continued to rule in the south, the new Fourteenth Dynasty ruled in the north. About 1650 BC a group calling themselves the foreign rulers, or Hyksos, took power. There they engaged in trade and lived the good life. They adopted

---

1. You have to wonder why. Looking for food perhaps?

some Egyptian ways and kept some of their own. Culturally, they were far more like the Children of Israel than the Egyptians were.

The weakened state of the Egyptians also allowed the Nubians south of Thebes to exert some independence of their own. The Egyptians had been keeping pretty strict rule over the area both with their military and their trade. They had a system of forts to maintain control of the region. When their influence waned, it allowed the kingdom of Kush to form. With their capitol at Kerma, the Kushites experienced a classical period. They had developed a culture similar to that of other east African people but also heavily influenced by Egypt. There is not a whole lot left of it to put in a museum[2] unfortunately since when the Egyptians reasserted control they destroyed almost everything.

The Seventeenth Dynasty was the successor of the Thirteenth, since Fifteenth and Sixteenth were foreign and Fourteenth only ruled a few years before being conquered. The Seventeenth ruled what it could at Thebes, sandwiched between the Hyksos to the north and Kush to the south. It maintained trade with both, but the glorious empire of Egypt seemed to be at an end.

Then the Eighteenth Dynasty picked Egypt up off the ground in 1550 BC. This Dynasty was born in war. It drove out the Hyksos, taking their new weapon, the chariot and using it against them. It took decades but the Egyptians finally drove those foreigners out completely. The Hyksos were similar to the children of Israel, but they were distinct. The Israelites did not help the Hyksos to take over, neither did they defend them from the Eighteenth Dynasty. Nonetheless, the Egyptians did not trust the Israelites one tiny little bit.

The Eighteenth Dynasty then turned its attention to Kush. First, it restored its forts along the upper Nile. Then it sailed down

---

2. Much to the sorrow of the British Museum.

the Nile, sacking Kush, burning the capitol of Kerma to the ground. It executed the king of Kush by hanging him from the mast of a ship by his ankles. Campaigns to subdue Kush continued until the reign of Thutmose III.

It is into this Eighteenth Dynasty Egypt that Moses, I would contend, was born. This is no minor point, as you will find out. I will defend this position in some detail.

Perhaps you have seen *Prince of Egypt* or the *Ten Commandments*. One thing those movies have in common is that when Moses argues with Pharaoh, he addresses him as Ramesses, a Pharaoh of the Nineteenth Dynasty. The reason for this is that much scholarly consensus has formed around the date of the Exodus. This problem with this late date of the Exodus is at the root of endless later problems when trying to harmonize the events found in the Bible with archeology. I think it is worth our time to look at the arguments for a late, or Thirteenth Century Exodus.

If you read your Bible, Exodus 1:11 clearly states that the Israelites were working on Pi Ramesses, which, scholars argue, is named for Ramesses. Now there is no evidence that the city is not named for that Pharaoh[3]. Yet it is possible that it is not. You see, Ramesses means son of Ra. Now that is the name of some of the Nineteenth Dynasty Pharaohs. All Pharaoh s, regardless of their name are considered sons of Ra. It is entirely possible that any Pharaoh could name a city that. The fact that the city was named Pi Ramesses is not conclusive evidence for their position.

In fact, it causes them some problems. The Ramesses they want us to think was the brother of Moses and Pharaoh of the Exodus was Ramesses II. Now the Ramesses, if the city is named for him, must have been tossing Hebrew babies into the Nile

---

3. Direct evidence, that is.

and building the city could only be backed up to Ramesses I. Assuming Moses goes into the drink on the first year of his reign, 1292 BC, Moses killed the Egyptian and fled into the desert during the reign of Ramesses II, 1252 BC, when Moses was forty[4]. The problem is, Moses waited until the Pharaoh who sought his life was dead to return. Even worse, Ramesses II's heir Merneptah recorded on a carved stone stele, which is on display at the Egyptian museum at Cairo, that before his fifth year he had won a mighty victory in battle in the region of modern-day Israel against, among other people groups, the Children of Israel. Even worse, Moses was in exile forty years before he returned[5] which would have him back in Egypt after Merneptah was dead. How is a man supposed to lead the children of Israel to the Promised Land in negative time?

Those holding to the Nineteenth Dynasty[6] view will counter that forty years appears way too often in Scripture to be taken seriously. They contend that you can use any period of time you like when it says forty years. Forty years does appear a suspicious number of times, to be fair to them. To be fair to me, it also says Moses was eighty when he stood before Pharaoh[7]. If that isn't good enough because that's just two times forty, it also says Aaron was eighty-three[8].

Those who argue for the Nineteenth Dynasty also point to the fact that Ramesses II has record of Apiru laborers on his projects. The Exodus must have taken place about halfway through his reign in order for the Israelites to be in place in time for his successor, Merneptah, to have faced them and mention them on

---

4. Acts 7:23
5. Acts 7:30
6. That ruled during the Thirteenth Century BC.
7. Exodus 7:7
8. Also Exodus 7:7

his stele. The earliest mention of Israel is on that stele as I have mentioned and is dated to 1220 BC.

Again, if you toss any mention of forty years out the window, like the forty-year wandering in the desert, you could imagine there was time for this. Let me take you at the breakneck speed that would be required. From the beginning of the reign of Ramesses I to the death of his successor, Seti I, we have thirteen years. Ramesses II reigns a further sixty-six years. That is seventy-nine years for Moses to grow up, flee to Midian, meet God at the burning bush, and have the Exodus. So far, not so bad as long as you don't get hung up on that forty-year thing. This also needs to include the conquest of Canaan and the occupation of the land afterwards. Remember, Moses has to grow up during this seventy-nine years and die of old age before they enter the land. The entire generation that refused to enter at first with the bad report of the scouts had to die as well. How long really does that give them to conquer the land? I don't know that I could grant them "plenty of time." Clearly this assertion does violence to the entire Biblical account of the Exodus.

The Thirteenth Century Exodus historian asserts that the reign of the Eighteenth Dynasty Pharaohs, who ruled during the early Exodus date, would not have been conducive to the Exodus. Thutmose III and Amenhotep II exercised suzerainty over Canaan and would have not have been so easy to escape. While the Eighteenth Dynasty was strong, Pharaohs of the Nineteenth were absent from Canaan and the Exodus would fit better during their rule.

Now, I have no idea what books these guys have been reading. Ramesses II was also known as Ramesses the Great. He was without a doubt the most powerful Pharaoh of the New Kingdom era. Not only did he launch incursions into Canaan, he did so while challenging the might of the Hittite empire. I counter that the ridiculous success of Ramesses II does not fit the story of a Pharaoh who got his kingdom ripped to pieces before his eyes. It is true that the Eighteenth Dynasty Pharaohs did have vassals and a fort in Canaan. Nobody said the Canaanites Joshua was slaying were not Egyptian vassals. They just weren't vassals Egypt was properly defending.

The argument for the Nineteenth Dynasty based on archeology is now largely out of date. No settlements had been found in the area where the Israelites on their Exodus encountered them during the Fifteenth Century BC. This argument is outdated, though, since almost sixty settlements have been unearthed more recently from the twentieth to thirteenth centuries in the Trans-Jordan region. There turns out to have been plenty of settlement at the proper time.

Now as ironclad as all of those arguments are for the Thirteenth Century Exodus, they are not the actual reason why people concluded initially to date it then. You see, that date is the one traditionally held by Jewish rabbis for the Exodus. Now I can hear you say that if the Jews don't know when it was, who can you ask? I appreciate that point, but hear me out. That date was traditionally held because they deduced it from how many years they believed the First Temple was standing. They then recalled that I Kings 6:1 gave the number of years from the Exodus to the building of the first Temple. The problem comes from the fact that they dated the destruction of that first Temple at 420 BC. Today we can be quite sure it was 586 BC. This misdating of the destruction of the First Temple caused the rest of their dates to be off as well.

Now that we have dispensed with the best arguments for an Exodus during the Thirteenth Century BC under the Nineteenth Dynasty, I would like to lay out the case for the Fifteenth Century BC Exodus under the Eighteenth Dynasty. First, I would like for you to consider this. Please place the name Moses in the group to which it belongs:

Nineteenth Dynasty	Eighteenth Dynasty
➤ Ramses I	➤ Ahmose I
➤ Seti	➤ Amenhotep
➤ Ramses II	➤ Thutmose
➤ Merneptah	➤ Thutmose II
➤ Seti II	➤ Hatshepsut
➤ Amenmesse	➤ Thutmose III
➤ Siptah	➤ Amenhotep II
➤ Twosret	➤ Thutmose IV

If you need more, and I suppose if that last bit didn't convince you, I have my work cut out, you should start by reading the section on dates. Once you have finished, come on back.

We start with the notion that the Bible, if you follow the chronology given, when hooked up with our own dating system yields a date of 1446 BC. That is in the Fifteenth Century BC and would have come during the reign of the Eighteenth Dynasty. This is indeed fortunate because the reigns of the Pharaohs match up exactly with the Biblical narrative in Exodus. It is funny how the truth works out this way.

Thutmose I was the one who ordered the Hebrew boys killed. Thutmose III reigned at just the right time to be the Pharaoh that Moses fled from, and dies forty years later. This would make Amenhotep II the Pharaoh of the Exodus. Amenhotep II fits well for more than chronological reasons. He ruled from Memphis in Lower Egypt, which is close to where the Hebrews were in Goshen.

Amenhotep II was also succeeded by a younger son, not his firstborn. Thutmose IV outlined on his dream stele how he learned in a dream that he would rule even though he had an older brother. This fits with the firstborn being killed in the tenth plague of Egypt.

Do you remember that problem with the stele of Merneptah? Those Nineteenth Dynasty advocates couldn't account for him encountering Israel already settled in Judea. That problem goes away with an Exodus a couple of centuries earlier. If the Israelites left Egypt in the Fifteenth Century, they had plenty of time to travel to Canaan, conquer the cities and move in before Merneptah arrived in his fifth year. It makes sense because that is how it happened. Remember, the Bible is true, even when experts doubt it.

But wait, there's more. There have been found in Amarna, Egypt, some ancient clay tablets dating from 1360 to 1332 BC. These tablets were written in the language of Akkadian in the script of cuneiform and were sent to Egypt by rulers of other lands. At the time, this was the language and script used to communicate between kingdoms. Some of these letters were from Canaanite vassals calling on their Egyptian suzerains to honor their covenant by protecting them from a group of enemies they refer to as Apiru. It seems these "Apiru" were running rampant, conquering cities, and taking land. They were doing this in the Fourteenth Century. The Thirteenth Century Exodus Children of Israel would still be in bondage. The Fifteenth Century Exodus Children of Israel would be in Canaan conquering the land like a bunch of rowdy "Apiru." Now, as I might have mentioned, the Hebrews were not Apiru, but they could easily be mistaken for them. I'm telling you, believe the Bible and it all makes sense.

Interestingly, according to this Biblically inspired timeline, Hatshepsut could have been "Pharaoh's daughter." You know, the one who pulled Moses out of the Nile and adopted him. There is nothing other than her being the daughter of Pharaoh at the right time to suggest it, though. Pharaoh had many daughters, but I just mention it as a possibility.

Even more concerning was the number of Hebrews there were. Somehow, the seventy[9] had grown to close to two million[10]. I had a hard time understanding how this could happen as well at first. Even with four hundred thirty years[11] that is a big increase.

Imagine being a Semitic herdsman or farmer from western Asia. There is a famine on. You are coming to Egypt to find food to survive with your family. You learn that the prime minister is not Egyptian, he is Semitic like you. He and his family have plenty to eat. Would you consider the idea of marrying into his family and settling in with your clan? You bet you would. Within a few generations these new Semitic people would have blended seamlessly into Jacob's family. A few generations more and you would not be able to find anyone not descended from one of his children among the Semitic people living in the Goshen region of Egypt. Even so it was an amazing increase. It would require large families and very low infant mortality. In their increase, the Children of Israel were greatly blessed by God. He was keeping His promises to the patriarchs to make their seed into a mighty nation.

Just like He promised, after four hundred thirty years, God freed them from captivity through a series of plagues. Once these plagues were completed, Pharaoh begged them to leave. It was effective, but have you ever wondered why? The whole thing is way too elaborate. God could have just caused Pharaoh to be senile or nice and let His people go. Instead, God chose to do a series of over-the-top, almost end-of-the-world style judgments on Egypt.

---

9. Genesis 46:27
10. Numbers 1:46 The fighting men of Israel are numbered at 603,550. This does not include women, children or the entire tribe of Levi.
11. Exodus 12:41

Gods of Egypt

*For I will pass through the land of Egypt that night, and I will strike all the firstborn in the land of Egypt, both man and beast; and on all the gods of Egypt I will execute judgments: I am the L*ORD.

*But Pharaoh said, "Who is YHWH, that I should obey his voice and let Israel go? I do not know the L*ORD*, and moreover, I will not let Israel go."*

The Egyptians believed their gods were the best. Their gods gave them the Nile to satisfy their every need. It even flooded on a regular schedule at just the right time for planting. The Mesopotamians had river valleys too but their gods were jerks, causing random floods that sometimes wiped out their crops and sometimes killed them by the thousands. The Egyptian gods gave stability. No, the Egyptian's gods were the best, no contest. They knew it; everybody knew it.

The Nile is indeed a wonderful gift to the people of Egypt. God gave it to them for their welfare, out of His wonderful love and kindness. The Egyptians did not acknowledge Him as God, neither were they thankful to Him[12]. Instead, they gave their praise to images like men, beasts, and creeping things[13]. By the time Moses stood before Pharaoh, the ruler asked who this YHWH was and why he would obey Him[14]. He was about to find out who YWHW was. All Egypt was about to figure that one out with him.

Pharaoh himself was a god to the Egyptians. He was considered to be an incarnation of Horus. It was his job to ensure Maat. Maat was the peace and tranquility of the empire. It was the truth,

---

12. Romans 1:21
13. Romans 1:23
14. Exodus 5:2

justice and cosmic order that were ensured by the rule of Pharaoh. This Maat could be seen in the stability of the empire and the regular and orderly processes of nature. The flooding of the Nile on schedule showed that the Egyptians had Maat.

You can see how important the Nile was to their religious beliefs and how it must have shaken them when this God of the Hebrews turned it into blood. Khnum, the cow-headed guardian of the Nile source, was shown to be powerless. Hapi was the god of flooding the Nile regularly and occasionally was depicted with frogs. Heket was always depicted as a frog[15] and was also associated with fertility and the flooding of the Nile. What was that next plague? Oh yeah, a plague of frogs.

Geb was the god of the earth and father of Horus[16], Isis, Osiris, Seth and others. He was the one who weighed your soul against a feather to see if you could ascend or had to stay down on earth with him. As you can see, he was pretty important. It would be a real shame if someone were to turn him into tiny bugs like lice or gnats.

Next up we have Uatchit, the goddess of the marshes. She was often depicted either with, or partially as, a snake. She was known to have control of the swarm. They were just flies, but the biting sort that made for a much more convincing plague. God took control of the swarm and gave the whole land of Egypt, minus the children of Israel, a dose of the biting flies. We know they bit because later in Psalms it says the Egyptians got devoured[17].

Before Isis was the most popular female deity, Hathor was. She was goddess of love and beauty but also of dance, music, makeup, and even beer. She was the wife of the older Horus but was

---

15. This is getting out of hand, now there are two of them.
16. This is the older one, not the son of Isis and Osiris. Also see above.
17. Psalm 78:45

depicted sometimes nursing Pharaoh. Sometimes she was depicted as a cow.

Ptah was the self-existent creator god of Egypt. He was the god of builders and the protector of Egypt. The word Egypt is said to be derived from the Ka of Ptah. This god of Egypt was said to incarnate in the Apis Bull, a bull worshiped in Egypt. Another bull deity was called Nemur. He was worshiped at Heliopolis and was associated with Amen-Re. Lots of bull worship going on in Egypt at the time. As we know, the cow population was next up and got wrecked.

Sekhmet was the lion headed goddess of war. She would lead Pharaoh out to battle and bring him protection. She was depicted with an Ankh, the symbol of life, because she was able to heal and avert plague. She wasn't the only healing god the Egyptians had. The Vizier Imhotep, if you remember him from the development of pyramids in the Old Kingdom under Djoser, was deified and credited with powers of healing. Their inability to stop a plague of boils put yet another W up for YHWH and another L for all of the gods of Egypt together.

What was the next plague, hail? You mean a hailstorm in Egypt? Such a thing had never even been seen in the land[18]. Good thing Egypt had so many powerful deities that could stop this unprecedented storm. First there was Nut, goddess of the sky and ancestor of most of the Egyptian gods since she was the wife of Geb. There were also no less than Osiris and Seth, both of which were major heavy hitters and protectors of agriculture. There was no way either naturally or supernaturally that a hailstorm could devastate the crops of Egypt, right?

Okay, so there was hail, but Osiris and Seth probably were taken by surprise by that one. Who prepared for protecting the

---

18. Exodus 9:18

agriculture from hail in Egypt? Leave that to Eskimo or Viking gods. Now, locusts, that Osiris and Seth could handle. These were not just regional deities; they were some of the main ones. Perhaps the most famous myth of Egypt was how Seth murdered Osiris, chopping him to pieces. After Isis, Osiris' wife, put him back together; he was forced to go live in the underworld while his son Horus[19] challenged Seth for the right to rule Egypt. No way could anyone get through their protection with some lousy grasshoppers.

Now if there was anything the Egyptians had, it was sun gods. Amun was their chief god. When a cult tried to change religions for Egypt, it was to Aten, another sun god. Ra used to be their chief god. At some point they just combined them into Amun-Ra. Horus was the falcon-headed sky god that was also associated with the sun as either the winged sun or the early morning sun. The Greeks equated him with Apollo. Hopefully you can see what a blow to the Egyptian pantheon a plague of darkness would be. Any sane Pharaoh would toss in the towel at this point.

Pharaoh himself could not maintain Maat. The great kingdom of Egypt lay in ruins. The cosmic order was not in his hands, or the hands of any of the gods of Egypt. Pharaoh himself was a god to the Egyptians, an incarnation of Horus and a son of Ra. Putting his firstborn to death along with that of every Egyptian household demonstrated the complete power of YHWH. It showed He could even kill one of Egypt's gods.

God passing over the firstborn of Israel formed a tradition that would be built on theologically until it pointed like a neon sign at the coming and work of Jesus. God claimed the firstborn of Israel since he spared them through smearing the blood of a lamb on their doorposts. They were literally saved by the blood of the

---

19. As opposed to his brother Horus.

lamb. We also got the Passover meal that served as the model for the last supper that symbolized the advent of the New Covenant later. This New Covenant had to be formalized with the death of a God, and not one of those fake Egyptian ones either.

8

TAKING THE LAND OF PROMISE

And when the L*ord* *your God gives them over to you, and you defeat them, then you must devote them to complete destruction. You shall make no covenant with them and show no mercy to them.*

What could be better than arriving at the land of promise after forty years of wandering? The generation that had seen God's wonders was fertilizing the wilderness. It would not see the Promised Land because of its lack of confidence in God. Now, God, in his faithfulness to Abraham, Isaac and Jacob would keep His promise. The Children of Israel would enter the land, and God would give it to them.

Before we move on to this conquest, there is an elephant in the room I would like to address. Put in blunt terms, what the Children of Israel were commanded to do on entering the land would be called genocide today. They were to kill every Canaanite they came across during the conquest. It wasn't a normal war; it was extermination.

First, the Canaanites, like the rest of creation, were God's box of Legos. It is His right to do as He pleases with the matter of the universe He has created. He is perfectly in His right as Creator to wad our universe up and toss it in some cosmic trashcan and make another just like it only more respectful[1]. This is not an easy pill for His creation to swallow.

This right was being exercised in the form of judgment against longstanding wickedness. God had given them hundreds of years to turn from their wickedness. When God promised to give the land to Abraham He explained that the Canaanites were being given four hundred more years. God had shown great patience and mercy even though, He knew they would only increase in wickedness.

The second reason was to keep the religious and moral practices of these Canaanites from infecting Israel.

What wickedness? That is a good question. I am glad you asked. The Canaanites had religious observances that were rather above the normal limit of moral depravity. Primarily, of course, was the practice of human sacrifice. Babies were offered to Moloch. There were also other gods that were worshiped by having sexual intercourse with the "priestesses" at the local temple.

You will notice that some of the laws in the Law of Moses have to do with making sure that the Children of Israel are distinct from the surrounding people. There were rules as to dress and grooming that would make Jews stand out. When God delivered them, He wanted people to know that these were His people. Later, after they were dispersed, these marks of distinction would

---

[1]. Think about that next time you are thinking about something else while your pastor is leading the congregation in prayer.

go a long way in making sure they continued as a distinct group of people.

"But wait!" cry the archeologists. "There is no evidence of this conquest." What they mean, of course, is that when they look at the remains of the cities there are no destruction layers that would back up the story contained in the book of Joshua. You have to be careful because what they really mean is that there is no Thirteenth Century evidence. By now you know that the entry into the land was in the late Fifteenth Century. The misdating of the Exodus mucks up all of the archeology for them. By this point, they argue against a position we do not hold.

The first confirmation is in the remains of Jericho. The destruction layer dated to about 1400 BC shows a destruction of the city where there was first an earthquake and then burning. The layer contains late bronze pottery and scarabs from Hatshepsut's reign which are strongly indicative of the date. Hatshepsut's scarabs were not found for a long time. There are also features of the destruction that strongly confirm the narrative in Joshua. First, the presence of large amounts of grain shows that there was no long siege but that grain was stored up in preparation for one. The fact that the grain was burned also shows that there was no looting and the city was devoted to destruction, both features of the Joshua narrative. Now check this out. The walls fell outwards, allowing for easy access to the city by attacking Israelites.

Now the fact that there is not widespread burning is trotted out as evidence against the Fifteenth Century conquest. What they fail to grasp is that if you read carefully, the text of Joshua only calls for the destruction of three cities; Jericho, which we just discussed, Ai and Hazor. It is difficult to know where the modern location of Ai is as it is disputed. Hazor, for its part, shows evidence of being destroyed at about 1400 BC.

The fact is that widespread destruction would actually work to refute the Biblical account. God promised the Israelites vineyards and fig trees they did not plant and homes they did not build[2]. If they burned everything to the ground, there would have been no homes or trees to inherit from the Canaanites.

Another charge that is laid against the Biblical narrative is that the accounts of taking the land are radically different in Joshua and Judges. If you haven't read them, there is a surface truth to that argument. In Joshua they enter the land and burn down Jericho. Then they proceed to smash two separate coalitions of local city kings. After they are done, they sit down and divide the land up.

In Judges, they proceed to begin trying to take cities and evict their inhabitants with limited success. While the Children of Israel march through the land in a big group in Joshua, in Judges they are smaller groups working to take cities. Each tribe is basically trying to take cities on its own. They have mixed results. Dan fails entirely and just heads north to take territory, leaving its supposed allotment behind.

What you have to realize is that Joshua recounts the initial entry to the land. Three cities are taken and burned. The main activity is making war on the regional powers. With the power of Egypt interrupted, the Canaanite kings are forced to form armies to drive off the invaders. Joshua recounts how they were unable to do so because God hit them with hailstones, drove them from the battlefield with hornets, stopped the sun from setting so nightfall would not hinder the search of Israelites for fleeing Canaanites to kill, and so forth.

Joshua 10:40-43 does not mean that certain cities were taken, but that the kings of those regions were defeated, and their armies destroyed. Consider the fact that in Joshua 10:15 and 43 Joshua's

---

2. Deuteronomy 6:11

forces returned to camp at Gilgal instead of inhabiting the cities. This pattern was repeated after the burning of Hazor in Joshua 14:6. After the events in Joshua, the regional powers were broken and those who remained were forced to fight to hold their cities, no longer having the manpower to try to drive out the Hebrew invaders.

Judges recounts the time after the land was divided when the tribes, with mixed results, assaulted cities in order to take them. We are treated to the early history of Israel, prior to the monarchy. That is, naturally, the subject for a later chapter.

9

ERA OF JUDGES

*But the people of Benjamin did not drive out the
Jebusites who lived in Jerusalem, so the Jebusites
have lived with the people of Benjamin in Jerusalem
to this day.*

Jacob went to join Joseph in Egypt in 1876 BC. When the Children of Israel returned to the land after the Exodus in the Fifteenth Century, the political situation had changed. Palestine was still a place of small independent kings who at least paid lip service to a larger power. The powers had undergone a change. The events of Joshua and Judges took place from 1406 to just prior to 1000 BC. This stretches from the conquest of the land to the monarchy.

Much of that change can be laid at the feet of the Hittite empire. King Mursili went on campaign and destroyed both Aleppo and Babylon. These two cities were the power centers of the time, and most of the cities in the region that weren't vassals of Egypt were vassal to one or the other. What really put the fox in the hen yard, historically speaking, was that Mursili failed to fill the power vacuum he created. Perhaps he might have, but he was assassinated when he returned home. This set off a series of civil wars that left the Hittites too busy to consolidate their conquests. This old Hittite kingdom would be done for by about 1500 BC.

Because of this there was a dark age from about 1590 to 1500 BC. Meaning there was no powerful centralized state writing things on clay tablets to let us know what was going on. When the lights came back on and records started being kept again, there was a new arrangement. In Iran, Elam was in charge. There was a Kassite dynasty ruling in Babylon. The Hittites were back with a new kingdom. Mittani ruled upper Mesopotamia and northern Syria. Palestine was a sort of competition ground between these powers and the New Kingdom in Egypt. None of them could take it without the others letting them. Nobody was letting anybody have anything.

There are abundant records of the dealings of these kingdoms. They sent each other letters asking for presents and complaining about the last set of gifts. They also regularly exchanged gifts. They sent each other royal princesses for their young princes to marry; everybody but Egypt, that is. Egypt refused to send princesses, and the other powers resented it. They got over it since Egypt had the monopoly on gold. Having Nubia in the pocket was paying off at this time.

There was abundant trade from which everybody profited. Most importantly there was trade in copper and tin. None of the powers had access to both of these metals. If you mix them in a ten-to-one ratio, you get bronze. This was the Bronze Age. No regional power could hold power without this metal for weapons.

Sometimes these powers fought. Mittani went to war with Egypt but afterwards they became buddies. Sometime during the reign of King Suppiluliuma I of Hatti (1344-1322 BC), the king of

Mittani was murdered. Two rival brothers vied for the throne of Mittani, Tushratta backed by Egypt and Artatama by the Hittites. Artatama's son murdered Tushratta in a bid for the throne backed by one of Mittani's vassals, Assyria. The Hittites took this opportunity to invade and turn Mittani into a vassal.

In addition to adding the lands of Mittani to his bag, Suppiluliuma also made vassals of Damascus, Qadesh and the Ammaru. For some strange reason, Egypt wasn't up to challenging any of this. With what turns out to be the Hittites' usual luck after a campaign, the returning troops brought back a plague that badly weakened their empire. They had to deal with incursions by their northern neighbors, distracting them from business in Canaan for a while.

Those Assyrians did not sit idly by. With the Hittites distracted, Assyria took Mittani's place in the group of kingdoms. During the reigns of Adad-Nirari I and Shalmaneser I, from 1305-1244 BC, the lands that belonged to Mittani were converted into lands that belonged to Assyria.

This set the stage for the rise of Assyria. I don't know about you, but Assyria was a shock for me in the Biblical record. The fighting was with regional neighbors up until then. The stakes are things like: "Will Moab remain a vassal to Judah?" or "Will Israel retake the two cities that Syria took from them in the days of their fathers?" Suddenly Assyria shows up burning everything to the ground and taking over. They did not come out of nowhere. Assyria was a harsh reality of life back then in the Near East. Little did I know years ago that Israel and Judah were fairly close neighbors to an ancient superpower.

Egypt, for some strange reason, had taken to diplomacy instead of warfare in the Fourteenth Century; it's inexplicable. It isn't as if their entire army, complete with chariots, got destroyed in some freak sea crossing accident, right? Trade and their monopoly on gold had made the later Eighteenth Dynasty fabulously wealthy. In fact, it had been sixty years since the Exodus, plenty of time for them to have restored their military. Still, for a dynasty that attacked everything around them when they began, they had chilled out to an extent.

A crazy thing happened in Egypt around this time. It started under Amenhotep III. He started equating himself with Aten, the disc of the sun. Nobody would have noticed so much but his son just took it and ran. Amenhotep IV changed his name to Akhenaten. He removed the name of Amun from his name and named himself after Aten.

Akhenaten then moved his capitol to Amarna. He literally built the city and then moved there. He filled it with monumental works to this Aten. He built a temple for Aten that was just a courtyard with an altar in it. Aten could not be represented by a statue. Aten, Akhenaten contended, made the heavens and the earth, the seas and all that in them is. He brought order out of chaos. The other gods were fakes. Akhenaten proceeded to persecute the other cults. He forced the priests to serve only Aten. The temples of the other gods sat desolate, growing weeds.

Much ink has been spilled about how Moses must have been influenced by this monotheism. Wonderful of them to come down off of their "Moses was a mythological figure made up by priests in Sixth Century Jerusalem" argument, I suppose. Do you see how important it is to believe the Biblical record? The Bible says that Moses had already left the building.

Does it seem so odd though that Egypt, after the wholesale crushing of their pantheon, might want to have a single god who ruled over all? Am I saying Aten is YHWH? There is no evidence that Akhenaten was doing anything more than patterning a new god after the one that had so spectacularly delivered the Children of Israel so recently. It is normal historically for cultures that have been defeated to adopt culture from those who defeated them. What I am saying is that it makes sense that Moses and YHWH influenced Akhenaten, not the other way around.

Monotheism did not last long in Egypt. When Tutenkhaten took the throne, he changed his name to Tutankhamun. He was heavily influenced by the priests. He restored the old cults, reducing Aten to just one among many. Later, during the reign of Horemheb, the monumental projects Akhenaten built for Aten were used as a stone quarry for the monumental projects of Horemheb.

Horemheb was the last Pharaoh of the Eighteenth Dynasty. By far the most famous of the Pharaohs of the Nineteenth Dynasty was our boy Ramesses II; the first two didn't last much more than a decade put together. Otherwise known as Ramesses the Great, he built so many things praising himself that, if he were believed, we would have to acknowledge his deity. Not only did he claim a host of structures he did not in fact build, he even claimed to have defeated the Hittite army single handedly.

The battle of Qadesh occurred in 1275 BC when Ramesses was leading his army into Palestine to contest Hittite control of the region. The Hittites came on them by surprise outside Qadesh, scattering the Egyptians. Ramesses then, if his account can be credited, drove his chariot by himself into the Hittites, breaking their chariot corps. The main account, as you might have guessed, was from a victory stele Ramesses made to commemorate his valor. The Hittite side is that the successor to the king involved, Muwatalli II, mentioned that the Hittites had won. We are left to judge for ourselves. The Hittites still controlled Qadesh after the battle, just saying.

Soon after this conflict, the Egyptians and Hittites concluded a treaty that pledged eternal friendship to one another. The treaty was meant to last forever, but you just never know what the future holds.

During this era, the late Bronze Age, the world from Egypt to the Mycenaean Greeks and east to the Babylonians was in diplomatic contact. There was abundant trade all around the region. Necessities like grain were sold along with luxury goods from gold to olive oil. Most importantly tin and copper, both needed to make bronze, made their way from where they were mined to where they were needed. Nobody had both and every kingdom needed them. It was, after all, the Bronze Age.

About 1200 BC there was a little thing called the Bronze Age Collapse. There were earthquakes and famines. Some people from Sardinia, Crete, Greece and Cyprus were forced off of their land and set out, mostly by sea, to find a new home. These " Sea People" wrecked trade and destroyed the Hittites. They also invaded Egypt and smashed cities in Mesopotamia as well. The disruption in trade caused more problems that it is possible to tell you. Whole kingdoms functioned within the existing environment of trade. All over the Near East there were S.O.S's going out and nobody to answer them. All of the empires, save Egypt, collapsed entirely.

It was a dark age until Assyria got back on its feet and started keeping records again in 935 BC. Egypt survived with some damage. Ramesses had claimed a massive victory. The Hittite empire was gone, but there were still Hittite cities and people. A group called the Arameans moved into southern Syria where they set up shop and took over. A group called the Chaldeans moved into the region of Babylon in southern Mesopotamia. Some of the Sea People settled in with the Philistines or perhaps were the Philistines, depending on your point of view.

The Sea People helped to usher in a new age, the Iron Age. It was learned that if you mixed charcoal with iron, you could get steel. Iron was abundant and nobody needed to trade long distances for this new, superior metal. The Philistines had this military technology which gave them quite an advantage over their neighbors, neighbors like Israel.

While Israel was cooling its heels in Egyptian captivity, the Philistines of Abram and Isaac's acquaintance inhabited five major cities along the southern coast of Palestine. One of these cities, Ashkelon, was a major trade city along the coast as one sailed to Egypt. It is clear the Philistines had more than their fair share of contact with the Cypriots and Cretans who traded with them. Their pottery was distinctly more like that found in Crete than it was like that of the Canaanites or Israelites.

Gaza, another of the Philistine cities, controlled the shortest land route from Egypt to the Promised Land. If you have ever wondered why the Israelites took the long way, this is why[1]. The site of Gaza was once an Egyptian fortress to defend them from another incursion such as that of the Hyksos.

When the Sea People attacked, some of them ended up settling among the Philistines after they fought Ramesses III. It isn't clear if Ramesses settled their survivors there or if they went there on their own. These Sea People, the Peleset, were already familiar with the Philistines living in the five cities on the coast. It seems they just moved in with them and became one people.

However the fight with Ramesses went, the power of Egypt in the region diminished shortly after the Bronze Age collapse. The Iron Age technology of the Philistines combined with the excellent position of their cities made them a fine replacement as a regional power.

---

1. Exodus 13

Meanwhile in Israel

The era of the judges is outlined in the book of Judges. It is a history of how God had given the Children of Israel a land and victory over their enemies, while keeping a number of important promises to Abraham. The Children of Israel made peace with the remnants of the Canaanites and allowed them to survive in the land. The Children of Israel had one job. God was giving them a good land and all they had to do was take it. They did not fully drive the Canaanites out so God told them that they would be tested with the Canaanite remnants.

One interesting case of failing to drive out the inhabitants occurred with the allotment of the tribe of Dan. While later the term Dan referred to the far north of Israel, initially the land they were to clear was not there at all. Their original allotment was on the coastal plains in Philistine territory. It even included the city of Ekron[2]. The combination of Amorites and Philistines proved to be too much for them to overcome, Samson's mighty struggles notwithstanding. As time went by, the Danites proved unable to keep their territory and were without a portion in Israel. They were finally forced to seize Laish to the north of Israel, which was inhabited by Sidonians that were too far from their main city to be protected.

Before he left, Joshua had the elders reaffirm their commitment to God at Shechem. They swore to serve God only and remain loyal to Him. Once that generation died the people of Israel forgot God and turned to worship the idols of the people around them. They consequently also turned from other righteousness to do wickedly like their Canaanite neighbors.

The blessings that Israel enjoyed in the land were directly tied

---

2. Joshua 19:43

to their observance of God's law. While they were loyal and did right, God blessed them with abundance, and they had nothing to fear from mortal foes. God had proven that no nation could stand against Him when He crushed Egypt and when He broke the Canaanite lords before Joshua. When Israel was unfaithful to God and did wickedly, they were plagued with foes that they could not face in battle. There were also famine, drought, and pestilence. The national fortunes were shown in Judges to be totally dependent on their faithfulness to God.

Unfortunately, the record in Judges is of continued apostasy[3] and wickedness followed by foreign oppressors. When the Israelites cried out in suffering, God was merciful and raised up a judge to save them. Invariably when the delivered generation died, the next turned to idolatry and wickedness. This began the cycle again. The pattern was for greater wickedness, more violent and long-lasting oppressions and for judges of less savory character as time went by.

Judges in ancient Israel were local rulers with a military leadership role. They arose at need to defend Israel from oppressors. The position was not hereditary and not even exclusively male. Judges were often times warriors or battle leaders who normally led one or more tribes in battle. Some, like Samson and Shamgar, were noteworthy for the number killed with their own hands. Other leaders, like Deborah, had to call in generals to lead the forces because they exercised civil leadership.

Military power in Israel was divided among the tribes at this time and any concerted effort by any one of the world powers could have easily conquered the tribes in succession. God's plans, however, are not thwarted. Even while Israel was being punished by oppressors, the great nations were otherwise occupied in order

---

3. It was a bottomless a-pasta bowl in the land of Israel.

to give fledgling Israel time to grow. Egypt, the traditional suzerain of the Levant, was not undertaking campaigns there now, almost as if there were something there they did not want to face. From the fifteenth through thirteenth centuries, the Assyrians were occupied with the threat of Mittani and the mighty Hittite empire was battling the Hurrian menace. Both were careful of overextending and wary of each other. Around 1200 BC, Sea People migrated into the area, smashed the Hittite empire, and fought the Egyptians. The Sea People were broken as a major force but neutralized Egypt's army with heavy losses.

As a result, Canaan experienced a time of independence from the major powers that allowed the nation of Israel to arise and coalesce. When the powers returned, Israel was in position to defend itself in its hilltop fortresses if, that is, it had God's help.

The time of the judges in Israel was a dark age as far as the major powers were concerned, so there is little to be found in monuments or documents other than the Bible to tell us more about this time. The Merneptah stele tells of a campaign in Canaan that mentions combat with Israel. The Temple of Ramesses III at Medinet Habu tells of a battle between Egypt and the Sea People in which Egypt claimed victory. These inscriptions do shed some light on the situation in the area. They tell us that Israel was established in the land in the Thirteenth Century.

Archeology shows widespread destruction layers in the Thirteenth Century BC. This has been taken as a sign of the conquest of Joshua earlier, but we have seen how that does not fit the facts. These destructions of cities are entirely consistent with the oppressions that Israel was experiencing as outlined in the book of Judges. This eliminates the need to be skeptical about the Biblical timeline of events and of the integrity of the Conquest narrative. Unfortunately, critical historians are slow to revise their interpretations in light of the fall of the settlement gap theory.

One of the challenges of the Judges narrative is that there are too many years mentioned to fit into the time between the conquest and that of the early kingdom. This means that some of the oppressions must have been running at the same time. This is feasible because the oppressions were localized and affected portions of Israel instead of the whole. A good example is the oppression that begins in Judges 10: 7. It states that God sold Israel into the hands of the Philistines and the Ammonites. The Philistines were located on the coastal plains to the west of Israel while the Ammonites lived in the area on the other side of the Jordan River. Israel was caught between two oppressors simultaneously.

The challenge is not in feasibility but in establishing a firm chronology from the text. What we can tell is that with an Exodus date of 1446 BC we can set 1406 BC as the Conquest of the Land and also as the time when Sihon and Og were defeated and their lands on the other side of the Jordan taken. Because Jephthah reasons with the King of the Ammonites that it had been three hundred years since the conquest[4], we can date their battle to 1106 BC.

---

4. Judges 11:24-26

10

RISE OF MONARCHY IN ISRAEL

And your house and your kingdom shall be made sure forever before me. Your throne shall be established forever.

The book of First Samuel gives the history of the founding of the monarchy in Israel. It tells about a time when immorality was so widespread that the sons of the High Priest, who ministered at the Tabernacle at Shiloh, were chief among those who sinned against God. Because of the widespread infidelity to God's law, the nation faced severe judgment. The Philistines were overrunning the country. Something had to be done, and soon, or Israel would be destroyed out of the land. God, in His faithful mercy, raised up for them one last judge who would inaugurate their first two kings; one that was after the people's heart and, when he was shown to be lacking, one after God's.

The account opened at the Tabernacle which was located at Shiloh. Here a barren woman was given a child. In thanksgiving she dedicated the child to the service of God as a perpetual Nazarite. This boy, Samuel, served God from childhood while the sons of the High Priest, Eli, polluted the Tabernacle worship with immorality. They, as priests, defied the ceremonial law by eating portions of the sacrifice, such as the fat, which were to be offered burned to the LORD. When the people who came to worship objected, Eli's sons threatened the worshipers with force. The sons of Eli also broke the moral law by fornicating with women who served at the Tabernacle. This action paralleled the common practice in the Canaanite temples of having temple prostitutes. Eli, the High Priest, did nothing to stop them. Clearly, the ritual service of God could not be left in the hands of these corrupt sons.

Samuel stood as a striking contrast to the sons of Eli. He served faithfully even as a small child. God spoke to him and revealed His plan to judge the house of Eli by cutting it off. This soon came to pass as the Philistines smashed the forces of Israel at Aphek. Both of the sons of Eli were killed, and the Ark of the Covenant was taken by the Philistines. When this news reached Eli, he died in shock. Israel's High Priest was dead along with his successors, and the tangible representation of God's presence among His people was in the hands of their most hated foe. For a nation that survived because of the favor of their God this was not an encouraging state of affairs.

The disaster was only skin deep. God was cleaning house. The cancer in the Tabernacle had been excised, and a faithful prophet now shepherded God's people. Samuel commanded the people of Israel to repent of their wickedness and put away their false gods. When the people turned back to the LORD, God delivered the Philistines into their hands, and they were subdued before Israel. Samuel proceeded to righteously judge Israel into his old age. Samuel's retirement faced the same difficulties as Eli's. Unrighteous sons were set to succeed their father.

The people of Israel called out to Samuel for a monarchy to rule over them like the nations around them. The leader would have to be strong because of the Philistines. I mentioned them earlier. They were a blend of Peleset Sea People and coastal Canaanite peoples. If you were to drop your paycheck on who you would bet would dominate the region, with Egypt on the sideline, they would have been your safest bet. They collected the profitable coastal trade revenues, so their army was well funded. They controlled the technology of making steel weapons and controlled who had access to metal weaponry. These heavyweights were taking cities and oppressing the Israelites. They had already sacked Shiloh and captured the ark. Even the efforts of Israel's mightiest judge yet, Samson, had failed to remove the threat. If the Philistines were to be challenged, it would require all of Israel under the command of a powerful monarch capable of moving without contradiction from tribal leaders. The sort of powerful leader that could do this was a king like unto the nations around them.

God's view of what a king should be and man's are in stark contradiction. The ideal king of that era was one who was fantastically wealthy, had a huge army, as many wives and concubines as he desired and numberless sons. He had to have the ability to use his power on anyone ruthlessly. Such a king would not put up with Philistines raiding his cities and would deal swiftly with any threat. What they wanted was a big bully to hide behind.

God revealed His ideal for a king in Deuteronomy 17:14-20. God's ideal king does not multiply wives, horses, or wealth. What he does do is meditate on God's word. God's ideal king does not rely on wealth, army or his reputation as a virile he-man warrior. He relies on God.

Saul was a king like those of other nations. He was tall and commanding, a natural leader. When danger threatened, he moved forcefully to unite the armies of Israel. He threatened to slaughter the ox of any man in Israel who did not report for duty. He moved the united force to the rescue of Jabesh Gilead against the Ammonites and won a resounding victory. He faced the Philistines and dealt them losses despite their military superiority. He crushed the Amalekites and all but wiped them from the map. Saul was a mighty warrior who was just what Israel wanted.

Saul was not what God looked for in a king. No mention is made of Saul multiplying wives, horses or gold, but his pride and disregard for God's instructions are plain. Saul was not a man to meditate on God's law. He defied the ceremonial law by offering a sacrifice when he did not think Samuel would make it there on time. He chose to spare King Agag of the Amalekites and choice animals for sacrifice instead of destroying everything in the city as God instructed. Saul thought he could modify the commands of God at his discretion. Samuel rebuked him for his pride and informed Saul that God had removed him from the throne.

The man mentioned as being after God's own heart was David. Samuel found David herding sheep, the least exalted of professions. While David was just a shepherd boy, the least of his brothers, it is clear from the things he tells Saul before his famous duel with Goliath of Gath that while his body was watching sheep, his heart and mind were glorifying God. God grew David's faith through encounters with predators that sought to devour the sheep under his charge. One lion and bear at a time, David came to put his full confidence in God. When David saw Goliath challenging the armies of the living God, his reaction was not awe or fear at the iron covered, mountainous professional killer, but indignation that this impudent fool dared to defy God. David immediately went about finding a way to be the one that might challenge him. Everyone else was hiding. David wanted the opportunity to shut that fool up. Neither Saul nor Goliath could understand what this shepherd had seen many times ; it was not power, claws or spears that won battles but who had God on their side.

David, with his reliance on God and anointing as Israel's king, was invincible in battle. While Saul continued to tower over his foes because of his natural size and skill, he was overshadowed on the field of battle by David who won because the LORD of hosts fought for him. In David is seen the principle by which Israel won its battles in the past and any they would win in the future. David was not alone at this time ; Saul's son Jonathan also won miraculous victories against overwhelming odds because he also feared God. It should come as no surprise then that when Saul struggled against God's choice of David as king, Jonathan accepted it and showed David favor.

While David was in exile to prevent being murdered by Saul, he went to live in the lands of the Philistines with his followers. He was made the ruler of Ziklag as a vassal of the king of Gath. It doesn't say so expressly, but it is clear from other accounts that he picked up a number of Philistine warriors that would be some of his most loyal. When his son, Absalom, usurped his throne, Gittites, or natives of the city of Gath, remained loyal to him and helped him reclaim his throne. It seems everyone knows about the Philistines when it comes to them being enemies of Israel, but this aspect of them seems somewhat less well known. They were also loyal warriors who stuck with David through thick and thin.

Now, time was that critics of the Biblical narrative would make believe that David was a fictional character invented by the Jews to give themselves a sort of national hero to rule over a golden age. Golden ages are important for national identity. Unfortunately for the critics, Canaanite writing was found in 1993. It was a bit of pottery called the Tel Dan Stele that referred to Judah as the house of David and Israel as the house of Omri. It is on display at the Israel Museum, so it is difficult to ignore.

Critics, never to be stymied for too long, argue for a very different David; a cunning David who usurped the throne with brutal efficiency. The accounts found in Samuel are slanted to apologize for David's rise to power and the violation of the ancient religious center at Shiloh to move it exclusively to Jerusalem. They also see the account as grossly unfair to Saul and the family of Eli. The struggle was between Israel and Judah, which are different nations united only briefly under David and Solomon. The accounts of I Samuel 1-15 are written to vilify Saul, the founder of the Israelite monarchy, along with his religious supporters from the Elide family. This slanted account, written to the critic's mind as late as the Sixth Century BC, justified Judah's dominance and claim to all of Israel as well as the exclusivity of worship in Jerusalem.

On the surface this argument is a good one. Near Eastern monarchies did write histories that glorified the ruling dynasty. The house of David still ruled Judah as late as the Sixth Century. The story of a good-natured pious man receiving power, for which he did not kill, does not sound like how things actually happened in the real world. David did not act a whole lot like most rulers. Most, once you got to know them, would sell their mothers into slavery to increase their power. Many had killed brothers or other near relatives to gain or maintain it. David's enemies died without his prompting. The obstacles to his power were eliminated against his will. He piously punished those who killed Saul and Ish-bosheth[1] then took power over their slain bodies. Without understanding the divine element this story makes no sense whatsoever.

Digging deeper we find some problems with this revision of

---

1. Probably not his real name. It means "man of shame."

history. Near Eastern monarchies did write flattering histories that extolled accomplishments and eliminated failures. Upon closer examination, this isn't the case at all with the book of Samuel. David, the glorious founder of the dynasty, is portrayed warts and all. His vile sin with Bathsheba is hardly glossed over or minimized. David's sin is detailed and discussed for the better part of two chapters. The turmoil and dissension in his own family is discussed in detail and included incestuous rape and fratricide. The Biblical account is slanted, but not towards David. The point of view is relentlessly God slanted.

After the death of Saul on Mount Gilboa, the kingdom of Israel was united underneath David and then his successor, Solomon. The account of their reign can be found in Second Samuel, First Chronicles, the first eleven chapters of First Kings and the first nine chapters of Second Chronicles. These reigns are given acute attention in Scripture and, I think it is safe to say, not for entirely historical reasons. Theologically, David's reign is very important because God gave David a promise that developed the revelation of His plan to redeem for Himself a people from every tribe, tongue and nation. That said, there is great historical revelation as well because, as with most of the rest of early Israelite history, it is the only written account.

It is not surprising that other nations would not write of the reign of David. The great nations were still busy with their hinterlands, and the small nations could hardly be expected to put what David did to them on their stele. David was a military leader. His faith in God's protection and power in battle had moved past the duel-with-giants phase, and now he was trusting God to deliver the enemies of Israel on every side into his hands. Despite his flaws, David was a ruler who exhibited the justice and righteousness that God required of His people. David also exhibited the same sort of faith that pleased God in Abraham. Army size had nothing to do with it. Nobody could stand before the armies of the living God. The reign of Solomon was peaceful because the nations that were not at peace with Israel were conquered or vassals.

When Saul died, David began the diplomatic work of uniting Israel from his throne over Judah in Hebron despite the succession war he was engaging in with Saul's son Ish-Bosheth. David reached out to the people of Jabesh Gilead by praising them for caring for Saul's body. David mourned Saul and Jonathan publicly. When Joab murdered Abner and when Ish-Bosheth was assassinated, David mourned their deaths publicly as well. With the family of Saul gone, David was invited by the remaining tribes to be king, and he reigned over all of Israel. The shepherd whom God had chosen was now to shepherd God's people. The wolf of the Philistines and bear of the Ammonites still menaced the sheepfold, but David had experience with their sort.

Saul, the king like unto the nations, had won victories and kept the enemies of Israel at bay. The Philistines eventually killed him in battle. David began his conquest by taking Jerusalem back from the Jebusites. David then moved against the Philistines in a very different way. Instead of keeping them at bay like Saul, he engaged in a slaughter of Philistines from Geba to Gezer. This engagement drove the Philistines out of the hill country by Jerusalem back to the plains. He took their chief city and put them under vassalage.

Similarly, when David moved against the Ammonites, they were brought to heel despite hiring the Arameans to fight against Israel. The Arameans were crushed, their cities reduced to tributaries. David placed garrisons in their capitol, Damascus. The Ammonites who hired the Arameans were not only made tributary, their population was put in national slavery. Now Ammon was forced to send workers to Israel to do David's public works. The Moabites were made tributary, their army executed down to a third of its previous size. They too were put under Israelite garrisons. The plunder of these conquests David laid aside for the building of the Temple.

The Sidonians sent emissaries of peace recognizing David as king of Israel and establishing friendly relations. This was the ideal God set out for His protection of His people. He just required their obedience. Future kings of Judah would be compared to David because he set a standard for leading the nation in righteousness. God was pleased to bless him by giving him victory on every side.

Military matters were not all that concerned David. Once he made Jerusalem his capital, he moved the Ark of the Covenant there. David wanted to glorify God by building a temple for Him in Jerusalem. God had other plans, but those plans included David. God made an incredible promise that the throne of David would be established forever. This was another unconditional covenant that God would bring about regardless of performance. This is fortunate because the failure of Israel to maintain justice and righteousness, along with massive disloyalty to God, would soon be evident. This promise was a further revelation of God's purposes which were found in the Abrahamic Covenant that referred to the blessing for all the nations through his seed. The seed had been narrowed down to the descendants of David in the tribe of Judah.

One might be forgiven for wondering how Egypt, traditionally in suzerainty over the small nations of Palestine, could let such a powerful nation develop. There are not even records of Egypt sending in troops to try to stop the rise of Saul's or David's centralization of power.

It seems that Egypt was going through issues of its own. Power after 1069 BC was divided between the High Priest of Amun in Thebes and the Pharaoh in the north. These were not competing powers. They ruled cooperatively. Even so, the Pharaoh was not as powerful as he might have been if he were in full control. He was more like the foremost city ruler in Egypt than an iron fisted dictator. The Libyans were gaining influence, and by 945 BC the Egyptians had handed over the throne to a Libyan Dynasty, the Twenty-Second. The new Pharaoh, Shishonk I, built up Tanis and ruled from there. This lack of centralized power also permitted Nubia to flourish, now out from under the boot of Egypt. Keep that in mind. When we come back to Egypt later, that is going to be important.

Solomon

The reign of Solomon, no less than that of David, has been criticized by secular historians as belonging to an invented golden age of Israel. The political dominance enjoyed, and the wealth mentioned, were just too great for it to have been real. The power and fortune of Solomon seem copied from the opulence and power of the great kings of Babylon or Persia. Where would wealth such as is mentioned in the Biblical narrative have come from? The wealth and power were at a high point during their reigns, but what the secular historians fail to notice is that the description of wealth and power under Solomon is not slanted to show him in a good light. We will look at his reign in context to see how this is so.

The great wealth of Solomon came from many sources. When Solomon took power, Israel was enjoying the benefits of the military career of David. The borders of Israel were at one of the greatest dimensions they ever would be. Nearby nations were either vassals or tributaries. Great nations, like Egypt, respected its power, and Solomon received gifts and wives from many nations.

Israel under Solomon controlled the lucrative taxing privileges on a long stretch of the international coastal highway as well as the King's Highway. There were only two roads that were taken to transport goods between Asia and Africa, and Israel controlled stretches of both. All of the land trade between Egypt and the Hittites, Assyrians, Persians and the rest of Asia was subject to Israelite taxation. This was no small amount of income. It was also why later Israel was constantly involved in the schemes of the great empires.

Solomon supplemented his income by taxing the areas under his control heavily and cut costs by exacting forced labor. Solomon had extensive trade relations of his own by both land and sea. He was a military broker through his control of the chariot trade. In short, Solomon multiplied to himself much gold. When the accounts of his wealth are read in this light, what seemed like bragging of the opulence of his power is instead a ringing condemnation of his rebellion against God's law of the king.

Solomon's greatest accomplishment during his reign was the construction of the Temple in Jerusalem. This temple was not the largest to be built there but it was made of the costliest materials. Solomon also built many other buildings in Jerusalem including a palace for himself and another for his Egyptian wife. In addition to the Temple, Solomon also constructed many high places for the worship of foreign gods. Solomon had numerous building projects outside Jerusalem including the fortification of the cities of Gezer, Hazor and Megiddo. All of this required an enormous amount of money. One thing Solomon had was money

It is not surprising that with all that wealth he would have an impressive army. His extensive stables and fleet of chariots are detailed. His control of this trade was a sign, not only of Solomon's wealth, but also of his military might. This military might was based not like David's on dependence on God, but on the number of horses and chariots he was able to field. Again, we see

Solomon's violation of God's law of kings. Interestingly, it can be seen that the conquests of David begin to fall away during Solomon's reign and his military encounters show no sign of David's success.

At the beginning of Solomon's reign, Egypt was respectful towards Israel to the point of giving a daughter of Pharaoh to Solomon, an unprecedented honor. Later Siamun withdrew his support and provided safe haven for Solomon's enemy, Jeroboam. Jeroboam, an officer over the forced labor, was promised the rule over ten tribes of Israel. The prophet declared that he would have to wait until Solomon's death because of God's consideration of David. The Syrians also felt themselves free to break away. A pattern is seen that as Solomon placed his dependence on the size of his military, God removed the protection He had given to Israel under David.

Solomon was also noted as having over one thousand women that he kept on hand as either wives or concubines. Just as David's disobedience of this aspect of the law of kings was damaging to his rule, it utterly destroyed the integrity of Solomon's reign in the divine economy. The reason for this is that it is written that Solomon's wives turned his heart away from God. Solomon's syncretism set the precedent for many high places in Judah that would cause the nation to stumble throughout its history thereafter. It is for this sin that God declares the judgment of taking away the ten tribes from his son Reheboam.

When the critics say that the reign of Solomon was an idealized golden age, they fail to understand the tenor of the passages in question. While his reign began well with the building of the Temple, the narrative relates how the blessed empire of David was reduced so greatly because of one man's unfaithfulness. Not only did he destroy the nation through disobedience to God, but he also divided it through excessive taxation and harsh forced labor requirements. These measures grew continuously more odious as the burden shifted to the remaining holdings as the Syrians broke away and because of the exemption of Judah from these burdens throughout. The ten northern tribes grew continually more burdened as Solomon continued his extravagant court life and endless building projects.

11

DIVIDED KINGDOM

And Jeroboam said in his heart, "Now the kingdom will turn back to the house of David. If this people go up to offer sacrifices in the temple of the Lord *at Jerusalem, then the heart of this people will turn again to their lord, to Rehoboam king of Judah, and they will kill me and return to Rehoboam king of Judah." So the king took counsel and made two calves of gold. And he said to the people, "You have gone up to Jerusalem long enough. Behold your gods, O Israel, who brought you up out of the land of Egypt."*

Assyria

A regular history would hardly take notice of the goings on in a small potatoes place like the divided kingdom of Israel and Judah. The history of the movers and shakers of the region at this time would primarily concern the Assyrians.

They certainly did have an effect on Israel. By an effect, what I mean is they burned their capital to the ground and dragged their population into captivity with hooks through their noses.

As David was becoming king of Israel, the Assyrians were reasserting control of their empire after a collapse. They mostly fought in the area of upper Mesopotamia to retake what they had previously controlled. Assyria was a militaristic society. The king saw it as his duty to go on campaign every year in order to please his god Assur. He was to lead the troops himself. He didn't really lead his troops every year, but that was the theory. The Assyrian battle plan was to enter an enemy domain and hit soft targets that were not well defended. Their army would commit atrocities in order to intimidate the people who were in the defended cities. They would then demand tribute, like a bunch of bandits, or they would demand surrender of the city in order to exert some political control.

Assurnasirpal II (883-859 BC) had a number of successful campaigns in middle Mesopotamia, moving towards Babylon. With such close proximity to Babylon, the Assyrian kings began to meddle in the succession and exert control on Babylon. He was also forced to build a new capital at Kalhu. The old capitol at Assur was too small to house the government of what had become a sizable empire.

His successor, Shalmaneser III, decided to get some easy pickings by raiding the small nations to the west. The idea was to get some tribute money. A growing empire needed lots of money and every bit helped. It was this expedition that was resisted by a coalition under Syrian leader Ben–Hadad. The Assyrians record the coalition at the battle of Qarqar. Hadad-ezer had the largest contingent, followed closely by Ahab of Israel. Arabs contributed ten thousand camel riders, and there were smaller forces from Egypt, the Phoenicians and the Ammonites.

Assyria was defeated, at least driven off, for now. The nations in Canaan went back to squabbling again once the bigger threat was gone. Assyria had to deal with incursions by the Urartu from Turkey. Worse, northern Syrian cities began to rebel, refusing to send tribute. Babylon rebelled. Eventually the city of Assur rebelled. The kings of Assyria had the next few years' campaigns planned. Remember, the Assyrians didn't conquer earlier, not because they couldn't but because they had bigger fish to fry and anyhow, they were just looking to extort some money.

Then Tilgath-Pelesser IV came to power. He had a plan for dealing with all of the rebellion in the empire. First, he diluted his officials' power by dividing it up. He appointed two men for each job. This kept any one man's ambition from getting the better of him. He also decided to expand the size of the empire through conquest.

Israel and Judah

I don't know about you, but I always found the actions and situations of the kings of Israel and Judah a bit inscrutable. New nations would arrive and depart. Some would stick around and become major problems. Sometimes Israel and Judah would be fighting and sometimes they would be helping each other. The information in this chapter is here to shed some light on these issues. There are big fish in the water and the waves they make help you understand the administrations of these kings.

First Kings twelve through fourteen gives an account of the division of the kingdom of Israel into southern and northern kingdoms. This division was set out by God as judgment for Solomon's unfaithfulness with other gods. As with many of the things God brought to pass, there were human causes that He orchestrated to bring about His plan for dividing the kingdom.

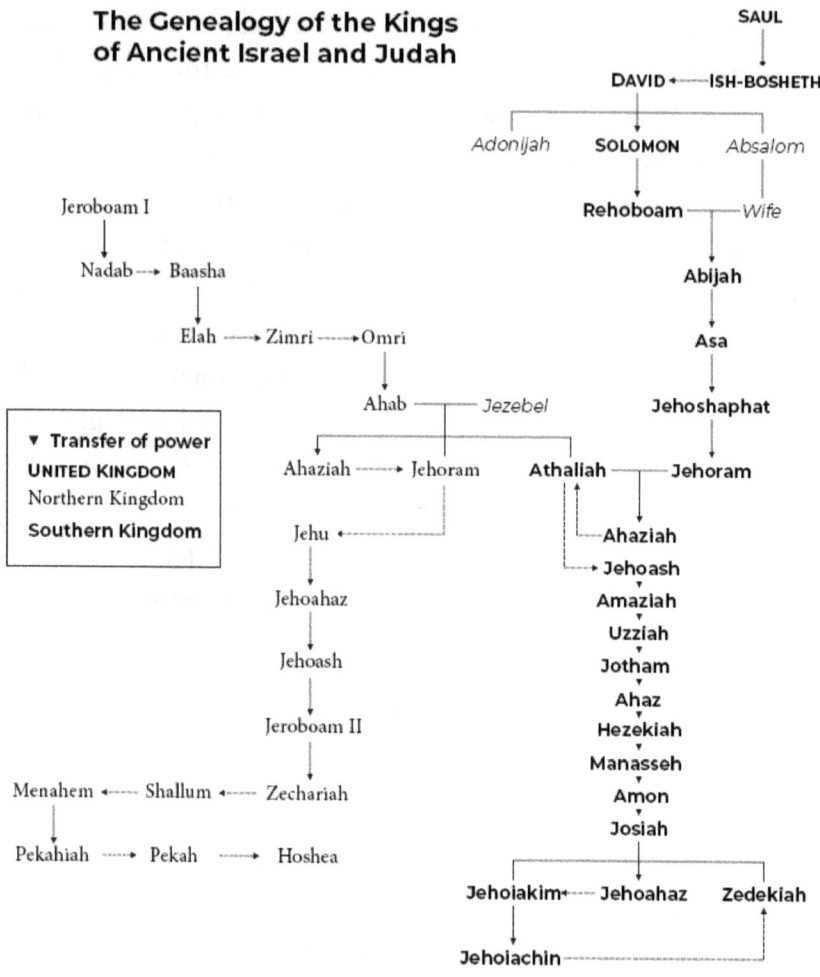

The geographical isolation of Judah caused a natural cultural division between them and their northern brothers. As Judah gained prominence under David, the place of Ephraim as a leading tribe was diminished. Ephraim had a proud tradition as leaders in Israel but many of the most important sites in Israel, such as Bethel and Shechem, lost prestige when Jerusalem rose to prominence as both the political and religious center of authority. As a result, Ephraim often backed rebels such as Absalom and Sheba son of Bicri in an effort to break Judah's dominance.

The popularity of the Davidic kings was not easy to break down because of the military accomplishments of David. This was a land and time where when you had a king who had the power to keep you safe, it was worth tolerating some heavy-handed government to enjoy his protection. The policies of Solomon were both oppressive and blatantly favored Judah. As noted earlier, Solomon's policies fueled discontent in the rest of Israel, but it was his inability to keep his vassals in line or deal with his enemies that made the Davidic line lose its earlier appeal. Clearly Rehoboam needed to show strength at the time of his ascension. His error was not failure to show strength and resolve, but whom he showed it to.

When Rehoboam arrived at the assembly at Shechem, he came to receive the allegiance of the northern tribes of Israel to be as his fathers, king of Israel. Jeroboam arrived and led the Ephraim contingent in asking for a lessening of the taxation and forced labor that Solomon had required. Here Rehoboam had the opportunity to speak peacefully with Israel. He could have given them some relief, or he could have set the agenda by promising relief in the future but calling them to aid him in facing the enemies of Israel, such as Egypt or Aram. Either he could have lessened the oppression, or he could have reestablished the strength of the Davidic line which would have given them reason to bear with the forced labor and taxation. Instead, Rehoboam ignored wise counsel and gave an answer that not only did not accomplish one of these objectives, but could only cause rebellion among the already disgruntled Israelites.

Critics of the Biblical account use this episode to point out that Israel and Judah were really never really one people and were united only briefly under Saul and then David and Solomon. They claim that the unity of Israel and Judah is a fiction created by the Biblical redactors and is presented to justify Judah's claim to be heir of the legacy of all Israel after the northern tribes were dispersed by Assyria. They go on to state that this is also to justify the centralization of cultic life in Jerusalem for all Israel.

There is a nugget at the core of this criticism that is sound. The division between the two groups was real and even from the times of Samuel they were referred to distinctly. That said, the implications drawn from this core are little more than supposition based on preconceived notions. The idea that the tribes of Israel are not really descendants of a common ancestor is really just a continuation of that line of reasoning. The difficulty with this school of thought, historically, is that naked supposition is taken at a higher value than written records of the time period. Even if your suspicion of the source leads you to believe it is the work of later redaction, the sources on which that redaction is based are records from the time period. As little weight as a historian would like to place on this source, the fact remains that the revisionist history proposed by these critics has no documentary evidence and is based solely on what seems to them to be most likely. Any such approach that replaces written records and documents with fabrications is not good history.

The split of the kingdoms politically led quickly to their separation religiously. Jeroboam, fearful that having all Israelites worship regularly in Jerusalem would cause them to eventually return to union with Judah, set up alternative centers of worship at Bethel and Dan. In language reminiscent of the sin in the wilderness, Jeroboam invited Israel to worship golden calves. He declared them to be the gods that brought Israel out of the land of Egypt. The locations of these idolatrous abominations, at the far northern and southern reaches of Israel, ensured that they were closer to all the northern kingdom than Jerusalem. Jeroboam also made priests of non-Levites and offered sacrifices to his idols himself. This caused the Levites to desert Israel en masse to Judah. There is no mention of a mass exodus from other tribes.

After the division of the nation, the Davidic line ruled only a small fraction of what it had possessed under David. Rehoboam's braggadocio cost him a greater rule and reduced him, humanly speaking, to a third-rate power. Instead of being bolstered by the northern tribes and drawing on their manpower, he was beset with a hostile northern neighbor. Forbidden by God to attack Israel immediately, Rehoboam went on a building spree, fortifying towns to protect Judah from Israel. Later war did break out between Judah and Israel but there were larger problems.

To the south, Egypt, under Shishonk, rose to prominence again and immediately proved to be a menace. By this time the native Egyptians were under the rule of newcomers from Libya. Rule was still not centralized, and Shishonk ruled only in the north. The account in First Kings fourteen tells of how Shishonk of Egypt carried off the treasures of the Temple and the king's house. The great wealth and armies that Solomon and Rehoboam had trusted in were of no use as God permitted Egypt to plunder Judah. The fortified cities that Rehoboam had built were taken nonetheless. The temple wall at Karnack reveals that Shishonk's campaign did not stop at Jerusalem. He continued north and, according to his wall inscription, sacked a list of cities that belonged to the northern kingdom of Israel.

The rise once again of Egypt marked the end of the period of time where God had turned away the great powers to allow Israel a chance to coalesce into a nation. The Assyrians would soon also make an appearance and would with increasing frequency menace the two small kingdoms of Judah and Israel. Not as large but much closer, the Arameans of Syria were centralizing and consolidating power. The time when Israel only had local cities and small territorial states to worry about was at an end.

All of this was exacerbated by the fact that Israel and Judah quickly began fighting over the hill country of Benjamin and Ephraim. Abijam, who succeeded Rehoboam, was successful in taking cities from Jeroboam in this area.

Jeroboam's house was judged for his sin and his posterity was exterminated down to the last man by Baasha, who founded his own dynasty to rule in the place of Jeroboam's. This was in fulfillment of the judgment on Jeroboam personally, that his line would be exterminated and remain unburied but rather would be eaten by wildlife. Baasha also did what was displeasing to God and his house was also slated for destruction.

Asa followed in the paths of David by seeking the LORD and refusing to tolerate idolatry. He destroyed the high places of worship and even demoted his mother from her regal dignity for her worship of Asherah.

In addition to the continuing war with Israel, Asa was also forced to fight another coalition coming out of Egypt. This time the northern Libyans brought Nubians with them as well. This sizeable army was turned back by a smaller Judean army in the state of covenant faithfulness to God.

Sadly, Asa failed to trust God when he was faced with Baasha fortifying Ramah to cut him off. Instead of relying on God to help him against Baasha, Asa turned to king Ben-Hadad of Syria. Asa took silver and gold from the treasury and Temple and bribed Ben-Hadad to break his covenant of peace with Israel and make one instead with Judah. The Arameans under Ben-Hadad invaded Israel from the north, taking the regions of Dan and Naphtali. This cut off large sections of northern and eastern Israel. Baasha of Israel was forced to abandon his building project in favor of concentrating on defense against Syria. The unused building materials were looted and used by Judah to fortify Geba and Mizpah.

This tactic, while helpful in the short term for Judah, was very damaging in the long term. Foremost was that it was displeasing to God. God had shown faithfulness to deliver the great host of Libyans and Nubians into Asa's hand in battle. The Arameans were a great menace to the kingdoms of Israel and while the war between Israel and Judah would soon give way to peace, the Arameans would continue to be a perennial threat.

The House of Baasha was quickly done away with. After an assassination and a civil war, Omri of Israel took power in Israel. Perhaps one of the examples that best illustrates the focus of the Scriptures as opposed to what secular historians think should be the focus of history, is the record of the reign of Omri. Scripture recounts how he killed the usurper, Zimri, and fought for the throne against Tibni. It tells us that Omri built the city of Samaria, that he was wicked and ruled twelve years. His rule is little more than an aside, mentioned only to make sure the list of kings is complete. Omri greatly expanded Israel's influence and military might. He made an alliance with the Sidonians, giving Israel access to trade wealth, and made an alliance with Judah, securing his southern border. The Tel Dan Stele mentions the house of Omri as being synonymous with Israel as David was with Judah. Without Scripture, his dynasty would be the first one we know of.

Omri's building projects were extensive. He built Israel a new capital at Samaria. The architecture from his reign shows a strong Sidonian influence. Sidonian trade made luxury items available, and Omri purchased large quantities of ivory that were exquisitely carved to build his palace in Samaria.

The Phoenician cities were not destroyed in the Bronze Age Collapse ; in fact they prospered. They continued to dominate sea trade and exploration. They founded colonies as far away as modern-day Morocco and Spain. They were still Canaanites and wicked as could be imagined. They fostered the worship of the gods that YHWH had ordered his people to wipe out. Friendship with Tyre and Sidon was lucrative but spiritually dangerous. Omri decided to marry off his son to a Sidonian princess named Jezebel.

The urbanization and population density of Israel at this time clearly showed Israel to be the more powerful and wealthy of the two kingdoms. Based on this it would seem unlikely that Israel was an offshoot of Judah. One might be forgiven for thinking that Judah was a hinterland. Even the defensive structures were more advanced in the northern kingdom. On a human level, Israel outclassed Judah during the time of Omri.

God's view is somewhat different. Omri was wicked, more so than any king before him. He was not worthy of note other than that he was another in a long line of kings who failed to lead God's people to be faithful to Him. He brokered deals that would bring the worship of Baal to both Israel and Judah. All that he did would be rendered useless as his line was eradicated by Jehu and his kingdom demolished by Assyria. The Scriptural focus on the southern kingdom of Judah is not based on these things. As was implied by the law of the kings, national wellbeing for Israel and Judah was based on God's favor. Gold and armies were explicitly not what it was based on. The treatment of the reign of Omri is consistent with the focus of Scripture and the values it expresses.

The battles of Asa and Baasha soon gave way to peaceful relations between Jehoshaphat and Omri's successor, Ahab. Jehoshaphat is recorded as walking in the ways of his father David and seeking the LORD. He established centers of justice under priests and sent missionaries to Israel to turn the wicked Israelites back to the LORD.

While Jehoshaphat lived at peace with Israel, he strengthened Judah militarily against other regional kingdoms. Both the Philistines and the Arabs were tributary to Judah. When Moab joined with Ammon to attack Judah, God caused infighting that resulted in their planned invasion failing without Judah having to face them.

In Israel, Omri the merely wicked was succeeded by Ahab the truly and sincerely wicked. With the help of his Sidonian bride, he actually outlawed the worship of YHWH in Israel and replaced it with the worship of Baal. Ahab's marriage also added to the growing troubles between Israel and the Arameans. The Arameans were concerned about the wealth of trade that the Sidonian ports offered. Most importantly, Syria needed to build a coalition against their eastern neighbor Assyria.

Now today we would not go about getting the aid of Israel against the growing power of Assyria by attacking them. Remember back then, though, that after winning a war, a new covenant could be forged causing the losing power to promise to aid the winner in battle. A number of battles were fought with cities being first taken from and then restored to Israel. This war chariot diplomacy paid off with Israel agreeing to join in the coalition against Assyria.

The high point of Ahab's reign, from the standpoint of secular history, was his participation in the battle of Qarqar where the Kurkh Stele of Shalmaneser III recorded him fielding two thousand chariots and ten thousand foot soldiers. This battle drove Shalmaneser back to Nineveh and delayed the conquest of the Levant.

Other than the brief period when Ahab joined Aram in facing Assyria, the record of the relations between Aram and Israel were almost uninterrupted war. Once the threat of Assyria was gone, the petty kingdoms returned to their squabbling. The Syrians were clearly more powerful than Israel militarily, but God worked to protect His people from destruction and gave Israel victories to keep them from being wiped out. When God delivered Ben Hadad into Ahab's hand, Ahab regained cities that he had lost but did not kill Ben Hadad as he was supposed to. This resulted in judgment and later losses for Israel.

You would think that his making peace with Israel would be among the things laid to Jehoshaphat's credit but the repeated admonitions of prophets tell us that his friendship with wicked Israel was not a good thing. The line of Ahab faced extermination for its wickedness. In order to cement peace with Israel, Jehoshaphat married his son to Ahab's daughter Athaliah. That wickedness then infected the line of David through Jehoram. He was recorded as being wicked like a king of Israel, which speaks both to his wickedness and the now given wickedness of Israel.

At the joint attack on Syria by both Judah and Israel to take back Gilead, Ahab was killed. His successor, Jehoram, immediately faced a rebellion from Moab as it attempted to get out from underneath the boot of Israel. Israel was backed by Judah and its vassal Edom. Divine aid was again responsible for victory. Moab was punished for its rebellion by having its cities looted and its agriculture laid waste. Syria continued to press Israel hard. Only divine intervention stopped a siege of Jerusalem by Ben Hadad from being successful.

When righteous Jehoshaphat of Judah died, his place was taken by Joram. Joram, if you remember, was married to the Baal worshiping daughter of the king of Israel. Now the infection of Baal worship had spread throughout both kingdoms. Lacking divine protection for his unfaithfulness, Joram's Judah was raided by the Philistines and Arabs who had given tribute to Judah under his father. The raiding was so severe that one struck the palace and all but his youngest son were taken off by Arabs. In his day the Edomites who had served his father cast off their covenant with him and aided his enemies[1].

---

1. This is one of the possible occasions for the book of Obadiah.

This youngest son was Ahaziah. His rule was cut short when he joined Jehoram of Israel in another assault on Syrian controlled Gilead. Jehoram took a wound while fighting and went to heal up in the company of his fellow king from Judah. God's plans to cleanse both Israel and Judah took shape with the anointing of Jehu as king over Israel. Jehu, a commander of forces at Gilead, took some men and rode to Jezreel where the kings were resting, and proceeded to assassinate them both.

Jehu was anointed king of Israel and given the task of doing God's will to the house of Ahab, extermination. After Jezreel, he visited Samaria where Jezebel was thrown from a high window to her death. Jehu then obtained the heads of the male heirs of Ahab's line. Was Jehu done? Not remotely! The cult of Baal was next on the list. Jehu held a high assembly for Baal's priests where he exterminated them. Because of his effectiveness when he wiped out Ahab's line, God promised Jehu four generations on the throne of Israel. In this way, God used Jehu to cleanse His people of the filth of Baal worship. He would take back Judah next.

When Ahaziah died at Jehu's hands, his mother Athaliah had his children murdered and usurped the throne for herself. Normally, this wouldn't be a good thing. The promised Davidic dynasty was within a thread of extinction. In a strange twist of irony, Israel was purged of Baal worship while the granddaughter of a Sidonian king ruled in Judah. All of this was according to the masterful plan of God. Unknown to Athaliah, the baby king Joash was smuggled to the Temple where he was raised by priests. The child of Baal worshiping parents was thus taken out of the wicked influence of the court and reared in the nurture and admonition of YHWH by His priests. It was only required that Joash become old enough to show himself, and the line was restored to the throne. Athaliah was frog marched from the Temple grounds where she was executed.

The Black Obelisk depicts Jehu's submission to Shalmaneser III. After Jehu's submission, the Assyrians became embroiled with rebellions, including that of the Chaldeans of the Sealands. After the death of Shalmaneser III, Assyria would be too busy to defend their vassal Israel. Deliverance would have to come from somewhere else. Israel had not maintained anything like covenant faithfulness, but God had mercy on them for the sake of Abraham, Isaac and Jacob.

Jehu was far from a powerful king and his submission to Assyria, while averting battle with Assyria, caused him grief as Aram took huge areas in the north of Israel and almost everything on the eastern side of the Jordan River in retaliation.

Jehu's successor Jehoehaz fared little better. His reign was a losing battle to keep territory as Syria continued to take it. The long fighting left the army of Israel in a sorry state. And yet, despite their evil, God delivered Israel from the hands of the Syrians so they were not completely destroyed.

Judah was faring only a little better as Joash, while able to rebuild the temple, was not able to resist Syria effectively. He was forced to pay off Hazael so he would leave off his siege of Jerusalem. This weakness and his murder of a priest caused men of Jerusalem to murder him and replace him with Amaziah.

Amaziah was a stronger king militarily. First, he had his father's murderers executed. He prosecuted a war against the Edomites who had rebelled against Judah in the days of Joram. His success caused him to decide to square up against Jehoash, Jehoehaz's successor in Israel. Unfortunately for Judah, Jehoash proved stronger than him. The result was that Israel broke down the walls of Jerusalem and looted it. Once again the failure of the Davidic king resulted in him being murdered by his own people.

You would think that the strength of Israel would have resulted in arrogance but Jehoash actually sought aid from God against Syria. This Elisha prophesied by having him strike the ground with arrows. The three strikes preceded the three times Jehoash was able to defeat the Syrians and take back cities from them.

Jeroboam II, Jehoash's successor in Israel, was yet more wicked, but he was able to expand the domain of Israel and break the Arameans to the point where he even took Damascus. The tormentors of Israel were silenced. When the mighty Tilgath-Peleser III of Assyria took power, the Arameans would not be strong enough to hinder him as he marched through both Syria and Israel to the sea. It turned out that with Syria out of the way, there was no reason to not just conquer Israel and add it to the Assyrian empire.

Fortunately for Judah, Amaziah had a son already ruling on the throne. Uzziah was also a righteous king who greatly expanded the influence and power of Judah. He equipped and organized a tremendous army complete with siege engines. He used his army to subdue the Philistines at Ashdod and Gath. He then built cities for people of Judah to live in on the coastal region that was normally under the control of the Philistines. Judah was respected and feared in the region. Uzziah also instituted irrigation and wilderness reclamation projects to bring previously unutilized lands into cultivation. His overwhelming success caused him to become prideful, and he was struck with leprosy.

The critics have less difficulty with the Biblical record of events at this point as it is confirmed through extra-biblical sources. Some do argue that Joash of Israel and Joash of Judah were the same person. This argument is based solely on the two kings having the same name. Strangely they are silent on the subject of John Adams and John Quincy Adams being the same person. Funny that.

The mercy of God truly is infinite, but so is His justice. The fullness of Israel's transgressions had come before God. The northern kingdom's people exhibited unfaithfulness and unrighteousness until they were even more wicked than the Canaanites they had replaced in the land. God sent prophets to warn them from their wicked ways, and they murdered those prophets. The time for God to judge Israel with the sword of the Assyrians was at hand. The account of the fall of Israel can be found in Second Kings.

Menahem took power after the disorder that followed the end of Jehu's dynasty and he stabilized his power by taking up a tax and paying Tilgath Peleser III tribute. This cemented his power by obtaining recognition from Assyria, which was in the land again after a hiatus. Menahem was fighting other Israelites for the throne and was not universally recognized as king. The renewed presence of Assyria in the land required smaller states to either submit or attempt to resist. Naturally, as long as Assyria had a presence in the area, Israel could look to it for protection. Menahem was a wicked king so relying on God for protection did not seem to occur to him.

Meanwhile in Judah, after Uzziah's death, Jotham took the battle to Ammon and returned it to tributary status. He was plagued by the alliance of Syria and Israel. This was because shortly after taking the throne, Menahem's heir, Pekahiah, was murdered by a usurper from an opposing faction. This usurper, Pekah, took the absence of the Assyrians as an opportunity to throw off the tributary status and renew the Anti-Assyrian league with Syria's king Rezin. At this point, Pekah joined Rezin in attacking Judah.

Jotham's heir Ahaz was dealing with a hot mess. Israel and Syria raided Jerusalem and sacked it. Edom once again broke free and joined in the looting of Judah[2]. The Philistines on the coast reasserted themselves and retook the cities in their area. King Ahaz chose to rely on Assyria rather than God and hired it to defend Judah. This caused Judah to become an Assyrian vassal state and had the further effect of serving as a pretext for Tilgath Peleser IV to take large sections of northern Israel, the coastal regions and Aram.

In Israel, faced with certain destruction from Assyrian armies, Hoshea assassinated Pekah. After taking his throne, he restored Israel to Assyrian control by giving fealty to Tilgath Peleser. This loyalty was only temporary as Hoshea sent word to Egypt to obtain aid in fighting Assyria. Egypt had been suffering from internal wars due to competing dynasties. Although it had emerged from those troubles, it was not in any shape to face a threat on the level of Assyria. Egypt would not be able to protect Israel just as Aram was incapable of even saving itself. The decision to trust in the protection of men had born its inevitable fruit. The die was cast for the destruction of Samaria and deportation of Israel.

When a nation submitted to Assyria, as Menahem and Hoshea did, it was permitted to keep its government and become a tributary state. If it resisted Assyria in battle instead of submitting it had its king replaced with a puppet. Unfortunately for Hoshea, Assyria had a rough way when dealing with rebellion like his. Rebel states had their capitals razed and their people deported. Once the original inhabitants were gone the Assyrians imported people from other lands to work the land. This kept the inhabitants cowed and unable to organize for the purpose of rebellion.

Shalmaneser V led the return trip to Israel. The campaign was very successful for the Assyrian king. He captured and razed Damascus, doing away with the resistance from Aram. He then

---

2. Another possible occasion for Obadiah.

laid siege to Samaria. After three years, Samaria succumbed and suffered the consequences of a nation that rebelled against Assyria. As a result, the land was soon inhabited by people from other provinces of Assyria who brought with them their foreign gods and customs. After God sent lions to chastise these idolaters, priests were sent to Israel to introduce them to the worship of God. Unfortunately, they refused to put away their old gods.

The so called "lost ten tribes" of Israel were not actually lost. Some remnant of them filtered down to Judah to return to God with the revivals under Hezekiah. According to the Assyrians, twenty-seven thousand two hundred ninety of them were resettled in Northeastern Syrian and Iran, in the Zagros Mountains. The Bible says the same thing, only in different words[3].

God had been exceedingly patient with Israel. Israel had its doom foretold from the time Jeroboam the son of Nebat caused Israel to sin with the golden calves at Dan and Beersheba. The unfaithfulness continued despite the ministry of prophets and divine mercy repeatedly being shown. Israel rejected the covenant continually, and it was judged and removed from the land. God still had a people in the south. They too failed to walk in the covenant constantly, particularly in the area of worshiping Asherah in the high places. The time for their judgment had not yet come. The instrument of God's judgment on Israel, however, was in the land and planned to do away with Judah as well. Unfortunately for Assyria, that was not what God had planned.

---

3. II Kings 17:6

12

JUDAH ON ITS OWN

Behold, the days are coming, declares the Lord, when I will make a new covenant with the house of Israel and the house of Judah, not like the covenant that I made with their fathers on the day when I took them by the hand to bring them out of the land of Egypt, my covenant that they broke, though I was their husband, declares the Lord.

For this is the covenant that I will make with the house of Israel after those days, declares the Lord: I will put my law within them, and I will write it on their hearts. And I will be their God, and they shall be my people.

Assyria, as we have seen, was a hard neighbor to have. They worshiped their god by going to war and had a tendency to crunch down neighboring kingdoms like popcorn at the movie theatre. Add to that their power and expanse and you had the superpower of Mesopotamia. They were not, however, without their challenges. It seemed like an evil murderous empire's work was never done.

For some reason Assyria would not add Babylon as a province of its empire. Perhaps it was just too difficult to rule. Perhaps the Assyrians respected the culture that had so greatly influenced theirs. Whatever it was, it didn't stop Assyrian kings from shoving their oars in to mess with who got to be king. Sometimes they would support a friendly aspirant. Sometimes they would set up a puppet king in Babylon. Occasionally they would just declare themselves king of both Assyria and Babylon simultaneously.

Sennacherib decided to go with the king-of-both option when he ascended to the throne. Two years later there was rebellion with a Babylonian Marduk-Zakir-Shumi II being overthrown almost immediately by Marduk-Appia-iddiha II, who hated Assyria. Sennacherib came south and restored control, driving Marduk-Appia-iddiha out of town to hide in the marshy delta. Sennacherib initially installed a native Babylonian puppet king but later replaced him with his own son, Assur-Nadin-Shumi.

Six years later, Marduk-Appia-iddiha took the occasion of an Elamite raid to nip in and kidnap Assur-Nadin-Shumi and hand him over to the Elamites. A Chaldean named Mushezib-Marduk took over Babylon. He then drained the treasury to pay off the Elamites and others to form a coalition against Assyria. It was to this coalition that Hezekiah showed off his treasures.

Meanwhile in Judah, Hezekiah was a righteous king who walked in the ways of the LORD faithfully just as David did. This king not only purged the idols from the land, he also had the high places and sacred poles done away with. He had the priests remove everything unclean from the Temple to be destroyed by the Levites. Hezekiah also called the remnants of conquered Israel to the Passover. While the land had been depopulated of Israelites, the remnant that remained in the land were invited to renew their covenant relationship with Yahweh, the God of their fathers. A great feast ensued and the proper worship of God was restored in Judah. Into this picture of covenant faithfulness and seeking after God, came the invasion of Sennacherib of Assyria.

Ironically, while Hezekiah was faithful to God, he was inconstant and unfaithful to Assyria, turning on them whenever it became convenient to do so. After taking power, Hezekiah threw off the yoke of Assyria and refused tribute to Sargon. Hezekiah then attacked the Philistines, who were Assyrian vassals. With the ascension of Sennacherib, Hezekiah aided the anti-Assyrian coalition that involved the Babylonians and Egyptians. The punitive Assyrian expedition threatened Jerusalem and Hezekiah attempted to make peace by paying tribute. Sennacherib had to head south anyhow to take care of some business.

Here was where Egypt came back on the scene. Remember Nubia? By this point it was in charge. A little back-story: in 728 BC King Piy of Kush noticed with displeasure that the Libyan Pharaoh, Tefnakht, was consolidating power. He marched up the Nile and broke the Libyan army. He didn't take over; he just did not want a unified Egypt putting the boot back on the neck of the Nubians. The Libyan Pharaohs did not take a hint. When they tried to consolidate power again, King Shebitqo of Kush crushed Bakenranef's army and then burned him alive. This time Kush kept Egypt. The kings of Kush ruled Egypt for fifty years.

Well, it was a force of Egyptians and Nubians under the command of the king of Kush whom Sennacherib had to go deal with. It seems that they were in contact with Hezekiah and had offered to protect him if he threw off the Assyrian yoke. They didn't win but, to be fair, nobody else that fought Sennacherib did much winning either; nobody but YHWH that is[1].

Both Second Kings eighteen and Second Chronicles thirty-two tell about an encounter with the officials of Assyria, who demanded the surrender of the besieged city of Jerusalem. Based on human reason and the historical factors favored by historiographers, the outcome was a foregone conclusion. Yet another regional power was about to be swallowed alive by the war machine of Assyria. The officials of Assyria pointed out these factors to the people of Judah. No other nation had escaped their hands. Assyria had an incredible army which even Egypt could not resist. Nobody was coming to their rescue. Judah had only a long siege full of starvation before the inevitable fall of the city. It was unavoidable. From a naturalistic standpoint, things should have gone much differently.

From the divine perspective, Assyria was up to its eyeballs in alligators. They had made not one, but two very big mistakes. First, they were attacking the people of God while their king at least was in a state of covenant faithfulness. Secondly, they blasphemed the one true God by ascribing to Him no more power than the idols of the lands that had fallen to them previously. It made little difference that Assyria was at the zenith of its power. It was of no consequence that Assyria was the world's superpower and Judah a pathetic tiny vassal state. Because of both His faithfulness to His covenant and for the glory of His name, Yahweh demolished the Assyrian army.

Naturalist historians that refuse to believe this account must ask themselves, why didn't Sennacherib take Jerusalem? The siege of Jerusalem was attested to by the annals of Sennacherib who recorded that he shut up Hezekiah like a bird in a cage. It would

---

1. And that's hardly a fair fight. Assyria just isn't in the weight class of the omnipotent Maker of heaven and earth.

have been simple to complete the siege and do to Jerusalem what had been done to Samaria. Would they contend that Sennacherib was moved by pity? Perhaps he wanted an armed fortress full of rebels in his dominions. The naturalist interpretation of history fails to explain this salient question but the Divine history answers it nicely.

Hezekiah led many reforms in Israel and was considered a good king. But his reign was not as flawless as it might appear. One fault that would prove costly was his showing the treasures of the Temple to emissaries of the Chaldeans when they were forming an anti-Assyrian coalition. This coalition was not immediately successful, but the persistence of the Chaldean resistance, combined with Medeo-Persian pressures, would soon prove too much for Assyria. Eventually Judah would pay dearly for Hezekiah's pride.

Another problem during Hezekiah's reign was that while he was faithful to God, the people were largely continuing in unrighteousness and unfaithfulness to God. The prophet Isaiah warned the people of Judah for their hypocritical worship in that they kept the ceremonial law but they clung to unrighteousness like abuse of power against the powerless and prideful ostentation of wealth. Unfortunately, the deep corruption of Judah would lead to the judgment of God. For all the faults of His reign, Hezekiah did seek God and God protected Judah. Unfortunately, good kings don't live forever.

The short-lived Chaldean coalition faced Sennacherib in 691 BC. It, like the Syrian coalition at Qarqar, was able to hold Assyria off. In 690 BC Sennacherib laid siege to Babylon and in a little less than a year took it. He burned it down and deported the population, as was the practice.

Manasseh of Judah succeeded his father upon his death. Manasseh, despite his later repentance, is remembered as the most evil king of Judah. He reinstituted Baal worship in Judah and even went so far as to set up Asherah in the temple of God. He was recorded as having practiced sorcery and permitted all manner of witchcraft and divination. He also sacrificed his children to Molech. His wickedness was rewarded by his defeat by Esarhaddon, Sennacherib's successor, and his subsequent deportation to Babylon.

Esarhaddon had it up to his tonsils with Egypt encouraging his Palestinian vassals to rebel and refuse tribute. After teaching Judah a lesson, he campaigned into Egypt and forced some of the northern Egyptian cities into vassalage. He faced Taharqo of Kush twice, taking Memphis, but left no occupying force.

Meanwhile in Mesopotamia, Esarhaddon ruled over both Assyria and Babylon, rebuilding the latter. When he died he left Assyria to his younger son Ashurbanipal and Babylon to his older son. This did not set well with big brother so he joined with the Chaldeans and Elamites to overthrow Assyrian control of Babylon. It was four hard years of war before Ashurbanipal was able to reassert control.

In Egypt, the northern vassals had taken the time of civil war as an opportunity to become rebellious. Ashurbanipal, aided by forces from Judah, Edom and Moab, restored control over northern Egypt, setting up Necho as puppet Pharaoh. When Nubia reasserted itself, Ashurbanipal campaigned the whole way to Thebes, breaking Nubian power in Egypt. By this time Necho was dead so Ashurbanipal made his son Psamtek puppet Pharaoh in his place.

Elam had stuck its nose where it didn't belong once too often. In 647 BC, Ashurbanipal sacked Susa, the capitol, breaking Elamite power and setting them up to be absorbed by the Medes.

Manasseh spent most of the intervening time in an Assyrian prison. After his return, he repented and did away with paganism officially and allowed only the worship of God on the high places. Even so, God declared judgment as having being determined against Judah for the reign of Manasseh. There was only to be one more righteous king and his reforms, while sincere, would only delay rather than avert that judgment.

The reign of Josiah was the last bright spot in Judah's history before a succession of wicked kings faced the judgment of God, resulting in the destruction of Jerusalem and captivity for the people. Josiah was a very righteous king. He did away with paganism along with the high places. He also repaired the Temple. While those repairs were being carried out, a scroll of the law was found. Josiah, when he heard the law read, trembled at God's word and rededicated the remnant of Israel and Judah to God. He held the feasts at great personal cost and with attention to obeying all the details of the law. As a result, God revealed that he would not judge Judah during the days of Josiah.

Critics of the Bible argue that the rediscovery of a scroll of the law was in fact the introduction of Deuteronomy after its recent authorship. They argue it was a reform document attributed to Moses to give it weight. Those who hold this view have several perplexing issues to deal with. First, why do earlier reforms, like those of Hezekiah, seem to also be addressing the issues laid out in Deuteronomy? Why would nobody contest a document's authenticity when it had no tradition as being an authentic work? As mentioned earlier, how did the Seventh Century authors of this script know to frame it as a Hittite suzerainty treaty?

Despicable deceptive scribe one: *"Better model it after the old Hittite form of Covenant."*

Equally deceptive scribe two: *"Whatever for? Nobody even knows about those anymore, not even us."*

Despicable deceptive scribe one: *"Over two thousand years from now we can fool people into thinking that this obvious forgery we are making is older than it really is."*

Equally deceptive scribe two: *"Good thinking. That was close. Such an obvious mistake would have been all over the internet."*

While Josiah rebuilt the house of the LORD, the LORD was tearing down the house of Ashurbanipal. The year after Ashurbanipal died, 626 BC, Nabopolassar declared Babylon independent of Assyria. The Assyrian king didn't do anything about it since who the Assyrian king was had yet to be decided. There was a hot little war going on over the issue, and the Babylonians decided to make the most of it. They weren't the only ones making the most of it, either.

While Nabopolassar picked off feuding cities, one by one, the Medes campaigned into the Assyrian heartland in 615 BC. It wasn't fast but it was decisive. Soon the Medes and Babylonians were joined by Scythians from Asia Minor in marching on the capitol at Nineveh to finish the Assyrians off. After they did, the Babylonians burned down cities throughout Assyria in revenge for their tyranny. The Assyrian survivors lived in tiny villages on top of the ash heaps composed of their former cities.

Josiah was clearly anti-Assyrian in his politics because when Necho of Egypt was traveling through Judah to get to the defense of Assyria, Josiah brought the Judean army out to face him. Judah was not a match for Egypt and in this case, Josiah's actions were not in line with God because He did not deliver Egypt into Josiah's hand. Josiah was killed on the battlefield. The Egyptians would return to punish Judah on their return from the fall of Nineveh.

Josiah's heir Jehoehaz was wicked but only for three months. Necho returned and established suzerainty over Judah and removed Jehoehaz, replacing him with his older brother Jehoiakim. Jehoiakim was also faithless to God and very wicked. He served as a pawn for Egypt until Babylon, under Nebuchadnezzar, arrived and exchanged the Egyptian yoke for the Babylonian in 605 BC when he defeated Egypt in a battle near Carchemish. Since Babylon and Egypt were now both independent of Assyria, they were just settling who controlled Palestine.

Just because they lost a battle didn't mean the Egyptians gave up. Egypt and Babylon continued to fight over control of the region until 567 BC when Babylon settled their hash. This is unfortunately well after Jerusalem had been reduced to an ash heap. In 602 BC Jehoiakim, trusting in Egypt, rebelled against Babylon and was punished by having the Temple looted. Jehoiakim was succeeded by his son Jehoiachin. Jehoiachin decided, just for a change, to try the rebellion against Babylon thing. It was a bold strategy and it paid off by having him dethroned and deported to Babylon in chains just three months after his ascension. Many in Judah considered him to be king still, only in exile. Nebuchadnezzar installed Jehoiachin's uncle Zedekiah, who ruled as a puppet of Babylon.

Zedekiah was also a wicked king, and he would see firsthand the judgment of God on Judah. He would also taste judgment personally. Despite Jeremiah's repeated warnings, Zedekiah trusted in Egypt and, I hope you are sitting down, rebelled against Babylon. As a result, Babylon besieged Jerusalem. When in 586 BC it fell, the city was looted and burned[2]. The walls of the city were torn down and the Temple was destroyed. A large number of Judeans were deported to Babylon, and the remnants were left with nothing but a heap of burned ruins. Zedekiah was captured trying to flee. His children were put to death before his eyes and his eyes were put out. Zedekiah was then led in chains to Babylon, his last sight the execution of his children as punishment for rebellion against God and Nebuchadnezzar.

---

2. Now to be fair, Nebuchadnezzar had been fairly patient.

Judah, like Israel, violated the covenant of God. Both were shown mercy and given ample time to repent. Judah, unlike Israel, had a promise to David that carried with it the promises to Abraham, Isaac and Jacob. God in mercy and faithfulness would work through the remnant of His people dispersed abroad to fulfill the promises He made.

Captivity and Dispersion

Meanwhile in the Zagros Mountains in Western Iran, the Persians under Cyrus conquered the Medes in 550 BC. He then led them into Asia Minor to conquer the Lydian Kingdom as well. With this considerable empire and a sizeable army, Cyrus eyed Babylon for conquest.

The Babylonian empire, although mighty, was short-lived. After supplanting the lawful heir, Nabonidus proceeded to neglect the empire and spend his time on trips to the desert. You would think that if you went to all the trouble to usurp a throne you would at least sit on it. He left the city of Babylon in the not-so-capable hands of Belshazzar. Nabonidus was unpopular with the priests of Marduk as he was known as a devotee of Sin. When he returned to Babylon after an extensive trip, he took temples from Marduk and gave them to Sin. Now, one of the fastest ways to make yourself unpopular with the people was to annoy the priests. As a result of all these shenanigans, Cyrus was seen as a liberator rather than a conqueror when he took Babylon in 539 BC.

Cyrus was rightly noted as a liberator. His style of rule was much more beneficent than that of Babylon or Assyria. He allowed people to move back to their homelands if they wanted to do so. He not only allowed people to worship their native gods, he also funded them in restoring their native cults. Cyrus funded the rebuilding of the Temple and had the treasury searched for the relics looted from the Temple of Solomon. He then ordered that these objects be returned to Judea where they could be restored to their purpose in the Temple. In human terms, you can see why the Persian Empire was more stable and less plagued by revolts than its predecessors.

The Empire was divided into provinces called satrapies. The native rulers now once again ruled their own people, under the Persian emperor. The deal was a lot like the vassal suzerain treaty on the surface; loyalty, service and tribute from the vassal and protection from the suzerain. There was one huge difference. The emperor could deliver protection, unlike most suzerains. The Assyrian heartland that had seen unceasing war for three centuries was as calm as a pond. The emperor built irrigation, and no warlord dared to destroy it. Cities were built and stayed that way. Roads were built to facilitate trade. If you live in America today, you are used to this sort of thing. Believe me, this was a real treat for the people living in the Near East.

The Persians did not give up conquest after Babylon. Cambyses conquered Egypt in 525 BC. Libya and western India were added to their lands by Darius, and Nubia was forced to pay tribute. What Darius is most famous for is invading Greece. We will leave that for now since it will go down better as the beginning of the section on the Hellenistic conquest.

Xerxes, in addition to invading Greece again, was the emperor who sent Ezra back to Judea. Ezra left from Babylon with special tax exemptions and a gift of gold and silver from the treasury. Xerxes guaranteed these exemptions in a decree that he sent with Ezra. This decree also ordered regional officials in Syria and Phoenicia to provide for the necessary sacrifices in the Temple. Anyone who disregarded this edict, Xerxes declared, would pay with their lives or perhaps a fine.

In divine terms, Persia was raised up purposely to allow Judah to be restored to the land and rebuild the Temple. Cyrus himself was prophesied[3] in the Jewish Scriptures. While Cyrus was convinced he had been chosen for his throne by Ahuramazda[4], YHWH is the one who appoints kings and rulers[5]. God used the time in Babylon to purge the remnant of Judah of its polytheism, a major factor in its exile. Judah had an opportunity to reflect on how it had failed to maintain covenant faithfulness. When they returned to the land, the Jews struggled with other sins, but the worship of Baal, Asherah and Moloch had been purged. Even in the adversity of His judgment for Judah's unfaithfulness, God remained faithful to His promises to Abraham and David.

The completion of the Temple was hindered by the power structure in Samaria. The Samaritans wanted their part in the Temple and the work of its restoration. The Jews, whether acting from pride or zeal for purity, refused. Both were part of the Persian Empire, so naked aggression was not acceptable as a method of solving such disagreements. The two sides resorted to appeals to the emperor which resulted in delays but also in the Samaritans being required to supply material aid while getting no portion in the Temple. The walls were hindered as well, with actual violence and treachery planned. The vigilance of the Governor, Nehemiah, and the hard work of the people allow them to once again raise the walls of Jerusalem.

There are many sources that tell of the Persian Empire at this time, including new ones from the west who interacted as enemies of Persia. The tiny province of Judea got little attention other than the Scriptural record. This is because it had become, in the world's eyes at least, very inconsequential.

---

3. Isaiah 44:28, 45:1
4. Some sort of ancient car dealership, I guess.
5. Daniel 2:21

The Scriptures were being copied by scribes who were beginning to form schools. They had exhaustive techniques to check and triple check to make sure the scrolls they wrote were identical to the ones they copied from. These schools had traditions and gained prestige from their work. While there is mention of scribes in the history books as officials, the reading and copying of Scripture scrolls became very important at this time for the Jews in exile. These traditions would continue and evolve into new schools throughout history until the time of Jesus. It was no small place in Jewish society to be a scribe.

In a relatively brief time, historically speaking, the nation of Judah was born and conquered. Now it was a small part of the Persian Empire. God's people lived in relative peace for the time, without the fear of foreign invasion. Some lived in Israel, in the land of promise. Others lived in Babylon, where they grew and developed culturally. Some still resided in Egypt, where they had fled to escape Babylon. Others were dispersed throughout the region. All this was also in God's plan for His people. Now that they had failed to rule themselves or to follow God through His law, a new righteousness would be manifested from Heaven, being witnessed by the law and the prophets[6]; a righteousness that would come through the Messiah.

---

6. Romans 3:21-22

13

PERSIA GETS CONQUERED

As I was considering, behold, a male goat came from the west across the face of the whole earth, without touching the ground. And the goat had a conspicuous horn between his eyes. He came to the ram with the two horns, which I had seen standing on the bank of the canal, and he ran at him in his powerful wrath. I saw him come close to the ram, and he was enraged against him and struck the ram and broke his two horns. And the ram had no power to stand before him, but he cast him down to the ground and trampled on him. And there was no one who could rescue the ram from his power. Then the goat became exceedingly great, but when he was strong, the great horn was broken, and instead of it there came up four conspicuous horns toward the four winds of heaven.

The voice of God through prophecy had come to an end until Messiah came, but history rolled on. The world of the Old Testament Jews, some back in the land under foreign rule, must change into the Rome-dominated world of the New Testament. A great many changes needed to take place in those four hundred years. The area must come under the rule of the Greeks, gain independence, and then be taken over in turn by the Romans.

As I promised, we will talk about Darius and the Greeks. You should know that almost all of this information comes from the Greeks. They cast it in the light of freedom against tyranny; the Republic against the Empire. Mighty free men fighting against slaves because they would rather be dead than join them in their slavery. The reality is that neither Persia nor Greece fit those roles exactly.

Since we already looked at the relatively light rule of the Persians, and how Judea preferred them to any political situation since self-rule, we shall look at Greece a bit. It is true that some Greek cities were democracies. Today we would look on them more as fairly broad oligarchies. In many cases, over half the population could not vote. Most of the time, it was much more than half that could not vote. I am not just talking about women either. Large sections of the population were slaves. Many more were residents but not citizens. It was a step in the direction of democracy, perhaps, but let us be realistic. Many other Greek cities were kingdoms still. Some, like the Spartans, were oppressive to even their male citizen population.

In 490 BC Darius had had all of the Athenian meddling in his territories he was going to tolerate. He had a brief and disappointing campaign in Greece in which he learned something he ought to have taken to heart more firmly. He discovered the superiority of hoplite formation warfare to his own methods.

Sadly, Xerxes thought that this situation could be remedied by bringing a much larger army. Ten years later he suffered some pretty nasty losses considering the numbers. He made it to Athens and burned down the city. The Athenians had made it to safety and repaid him by burning down his fleet. Those boats had Xerxes' huge armies' food supply. When the Persians went looking for food, the Spartans avenged their king Leonidas[1] by hunting down Persian troops and slaughtering them.

After this the Persians decided to deal with the Greeks by hiring them to kill each other. It kept them out of their hair. They needed them out of their hair since Egypt decided to fight for independence. The Egyptians even had independence from 404-343 BC.

The Greeks decided to put together a mutual defense force called the Delian League. Everyone was supposed to send troops to help fight Persia should they ever poke their heads back into Greece. Athens was in charge, because of course they were. Athens told the other cities that they could send money instead of troops and Athens would take care of the rest. So, it turns out that the other cities paid Athens to make a big army and lord it over them. Just like that they had an Athenian Empire called the Delian League.

Sparta did not like the arrangement at all and gathered cities in opposition to Athens. There followed a brouhaha that drew every city in Greece into the conflict whether they liked it or not. If people didn't like their king, they could get troops to overthrow him by telling Sparta that he supported Athens. If someone didn't like his neighbor, he could kill him and tell his pro-Athenian king that the man was for Sparta. Athens executed entire city popula-

---

1. Who fell in the Battle of Thermopylae.

for not choosing sides. They reasoned that might makes right. It was just that ugly.

Athens couldn't face Sparta on land, and Athens enjoyed the advantage at sea. With as many islands as there were, it evened out. Eventually Sparta was declared the winner. By winner, of course, I mean broken slightly less. Other cities such as Thebes (not the one in Egypt) rose to prominence to compete for power in the region. This balance of power was broken by a brilliant king of Macedonia who used reforms in the military and politics to dominate Greece.

When Philip came down with a bad case of being murdered, his son Alexander came to power. When Alexander told the Greeks that they were to accompany him on a conquest of Persia, Thebes refused. Now, Thebes was thought of as a lackey of Persia since the second Persian War. Alexander burned down that city and sold its population into slavery. After that, everyone was willing to go along with whatever Alexander was planning.

The new and improved Macedonian hoplite phalanx army Phillip had developed and some of the finest cavalry to be found in the world at the time accompanied Alexander on a rampage of conquest that would radically change the Near East. It included the defeat of the Persian Empire, but it was not limited to just taking on Darius III twice in the open field. Alexander also besieged and took many cities. One such city that took a lot of besieging was Tyre[2].

When Alexander moved into the region of Judea to besiege Tyre, he called on the Jews to send him aid. They respectfully declined, saying they had sworn an oath to Persia and would not break it. His response was that they would soon learn to whom they should be swearing oaths. The Samaritans, a group of people

---

2. Isaiah 23, Ezekiel 26

descended from the remnants of the northern kingdom of Israel and the people resettled there by Assyria, sent a force of men to aid Alexander.

When Alexander marched on Jerusalem, he found the priests proceeding in full clerical regalia out to meet him. Instead of slaughtering them, as was expected, he greeted them and took a tour of the Temple. They showed him a passage of Scripture that prophesied his coming[3]. They even did a sacrifice to God on his behalf. When asked about his behavior, Alexander related how he had a vision in his dreams when he was wondering if he should invade Persia. The vision was of the priests, dressed just as they were and the message was: "Conquer Persia without delay."

Alexander concluded his visit to Jerusalem by decreeing that Jews were permitted to live by their law, wherever they lived throughout the Empire. Josephus stated that as he was leaving, the Samaritans asked for the same consideration. They also asked him to fund the building of a temple on Mount Gerizim. Archeological studies suggest that the temple on Gerizim had at least been begun by Sanballat[4]. A larger temple was constructed there in the Second Century BC. The Samaritan temple and priests served as religious rivals to the Jews, particularly during the Hellenistic[5] Period.

Alexander decided he would rule in a similar manner to the Persian emperors. He did them one better by becoming the local ruler wherever he went. In Egypt, he took an Egyptian throne name, becoming Pharaoh. In Persia he buried Darius III after he was assassinated, making himself a member of the Achaemenid family. He conquered all of the Persian Empire along with Mace-

---

3. Daniel 8: 5-8, 21-22
4. The villain from the book of Nehemiah.
5. When the Greek speaking people ruled.

Greece and western India. Twelve years after he had begun, the army refused to go any further than India, and he returned to rule over his new Empire.

Who knows what would have happened if his rule had been as enlightened as his conquest had been efficient? Alexander was dead within the year of the end of his conquests. His son was still a small child[6]. Instead of honoring his memory and line, his generals divided up his Empire and immediately began using all of those state-of-the-art military forces in their respective efforts to take over the world for themselves.

The hottest piece of real estate was of course Macedonia. Lysomachus, Cassander and Antigonus fought tooth and nail over it. Cassander and Antigonus both died in the fighting but Antigonus' family set up the Antigonid dynasty in Macedonia.

When the dust settled Lysomachus ruled in Asia Minor. He was betrayed in 282 BC by one of his lieutenants, Philetaerus, and died. Philetaerus had made a deal with Seleucius I, the successor in Asia. When Seleucius went about his business, Philetaerus founded the short lived Attalid dynasty in Pergamon in modern day Turkey.

The ones that mostly concern us though are the Seleucids and the Ptolemys. Seleucius set up his empire in Mesopotamia and eastward but quickly started moving westward. Ptolemy took over Egypt, making himself Pharaoh. He also had Syria and Palestine. These two lines had a long series of wars primarily for control of Palestine. The Ptolemy s are just named Ptolemy with a number so they are easy to remember. The Seleucid rulers alternate between Seleucius and Antiochus.

The First Syrian War was pretty straightforward. Antiochus I decided to expand into Syria and Palestine, Ptolemy II didn't mean

---

6. Small children of conquerors have a way of disappearing.

to let him. In 271 BC Ptolemy held off his Seleucid enemy. End of war? Nope, just a few years to reload.

In 260 BC Antiochus II launched an invasion with the help of the Antigonids against Ptolemy II. Ptolemy lost some of his power in the Aegean Sea and settled matters with Antiochus by giving him his daughter, Berenice, to marry in 248 BC. This is where things got weird. You see, Antiochus II was already married. He gave his old wife, Laodice[7], some land around Ephesus as a consolation prize.

There are a number of ways a woman can deal with such a situation. You can forgive, even if it is hard. You can move on, realizing he never really deserved you. Laodice decided on option three, revenge. She seduced Antiochus away from his new wife and killed him with poison.

Now the Seleucids were down one king and the question was: "Who should rule in the place of the murdered Antiochus?" Laodice was of the opinion that her son, Seleucius II[8] should take precedence over the infant son of Berenice. Berenice's point of view was that her brother was Pharaoh. When he arrived, he could, and would, settle the matter. Unfortunately for Berenice, Laodice didn't wait for Ptolemy III to arrive. She just had both Berenice and her infant son murdered.

This lead directly to the Third Syrian War where Ptolemy III sacked and looted his way through the Seleucid domains to no small extent. He reached as far as Babylon and forced Seleucius II to give up land on the coast of Syria for peace.

Twenty years later Antiochus III decided to use the perceived weakness of the Egyptian monarchy to take back the land they had lost in the past to Egypt. He started alright when he took Tyre

---

7. Guess which city in Asia Minor is named for her.
8. He already has a throne name and everything.

and Acre, but when he delayed his invasion of Egypt, it gave them time to prepare. What the Ptolemys prepared was a huge army of native Egyptians trained in phalanx warfare that they proceeded to use on Antiochus' army at the battle of Raphia. Ptolemy IV not only maintained his land but took some extra.

Antiochus III was down, but he wasn't out. Fifteen years after his first attempt was crushed, he went in for round two. The Ptolemys were dealing with internal rebellion and were going through scheming regents for the child king Ptolemy V at a ruinous rate. No sooner did one poison the last to take power that he would get strangled by an angry mob. Certainly nothing could stop Antiochus from taking Syria and Palestine this time. Just to make sure, he convinced the Antigonids of Macedonia to attack too.

Well, the Antigonids were a wash because Rome decided to distract them by having the Second Macedonian War with them. Antiochus did a lot better. He beat the Ptolemy armies so convincingly that Rome sent word that he was not to invade Egypt itself. Rome had a vested interest in stability in Egypt since much of the grain that fed the Romans was grown in Egypt. That was fine; Antiochus just wanted Syria and Palestine anyhow. The Fifth Syrian War ended with Ptolemy giving up Syria and Palestine and agreeing to marry Antiochus' daughter Cleopatra. Yes, that is how Cleopatra[9] got to Egypt.

Included in the new lands taken were the important port of Pan, later renamed Caesarea Philippi, and Judah. This transfer of ownership had mixed reviews. There is a story of Ptolemy I taking captives from Judah into Egypt against their will. On the other hand, Ptolemy II paid out of his own pocket to redeem one hundred thousand Jews from slavery. He also gave lavish gifts to

---

9. Ancestor of Elizabeth Taylor.

the priests in Jerusalem in return for their allowing him to translate the law scrolls and add them to his library.

Antiochus' plan, no doubt, was to have Cleopatra guide Ptolemy V into becoming a sort of vassal of the Seleucid Empire. Instead, she looked to the interests of her husband and urged him to make a treaty with Rome.

Speaking of the Romans, Antiochus had decided that they were next. Rome had been meddling in Greece and had beaten up his Antigonid allies. Hannibal[10] had taken up residence in Antiochus' court and was offering his services against Rome. When Antiochus crossed the Hellespont to "liberate" Greece from their control, Rome defeated him decisively at Thermopylae. Rome then smashed Antiochus' fleet and beat him again at Magnesia in Asia Minor.

Antiochus was forced to agree to a humiliating treaty where he surrendered all claims in the Aegean and Asia Minor. This would not be the last time a Seleucid was humiliated by Rome.

---

10. Yes, the one who caused Rome so much trouble with his elephants.

14

WESTERN CULTURE

Now while Paul was waiting for them at Athens, his spirit was provoked within him as he saw that the city was full of idols. So he reasoned in the synagogue with the Jews and the devout persons, and in the marketplace every day with those who happened to be there. Some of the Epicurean and Stoic philosophers also conversed with him. And some said, "What does this babbler wish to say?" Others said, "He seems to be a preacher of foreign divinities" —because he was preaching Jesus and the resurrection.

Greek Culture

The effect of Alexander's conquest on the Near East could, like the importance of knowing history for Bible study, be overstated. "The ignorant western Asians were suddenly exposed to the magnificent light of Hellenic civilization" would be a fine example. That said, Alexander picked up a great deal from the Persian Empire that he incorporated into his own. The impact of Greek conquest was enormous.

The Greeks had developed a civilization based on building up the citizens with education, rigorous exercise and philosophy. Citizenship included not nearly everybody, but it included a much larger proportion of the population than were educated and built up in the neighboring societies. Many of the Greek cities were democracies. In those cities it was normal for young men to learn to speak persuasively and use their leisure time on intellectual pursuits. Even after they were conquered by the Romans, these aspects of their culture would endure, as they would be adopted almost wholesale by the conquerors.

The Greeks emphasized rhetoric, or the ability to speak persuasively. They saw value in writing stories down instead of just telling them. The Greeks greatly advanced the idea of literature. They came up with Drama as a sort of combination of literature and public speaking.

Speaking of writing, you are going to notice that the history is going to get a lot more detailed after this conquest. To the previous sources of history such as victory monuments, yearly lists of achievements from emperors and clay tablets with lists of trade goods, we will add written history. The Greeks wrote history. Most of what they wrote is long gone but other historians, ones we do have copies of, used them as sources. As a result, the level of detail we can draw is greatly enhanced. Some events even have multiple sources so we can get something other than a one-sided account. There is the beginning of the concern that the true, rather than the most glorious, version of events should be recorded. It really was a step up.

Some Greeks were into math. Much of the groundwork for modern mathematics was laid by the Greeks. There were developments in Egypt and Babylon in mathematics, but the Greek additions took things to a whole new level.

The Greeks were also into sports. Many of the sports we have in the Olympics are holdovers from the Greeks. Physical exercise was important in their worldview and was expected as part of the education of a citizen.

Underlying much of this was philosophy. Thinking about what reality was and the best way to live were important parts of the public discussion in Greece. Human reason was exalted and thus they had all of this emphasis on study and understanding. This led to an environment of great intellectual curiosity among the rich Greeks who had leisure time. None of this, I would like to point out, led to the Greek rulers we will discuss being even a hair more moral.

The Greek language would also spread throughout the Empire. It would be Greek, rather than Latin, which was the common tongue through much of the Roman Empire. Having a common language over such a large area was unprecedented. It was also a key component in how the Gospel was able to spread across distances from Spain to western China and across people groups. The entire New Testament was written in it.

This conquest was not all puppy dogs and rainbows, far from it. It would install a thin layer of Greek overlords over native populations. Unlike the Persians, who allowed the native rulers to continue to rule as long as they were loyal to the emperor, the Greeks formed a ruling class. The natives were second class and not citizens unless they were lucky. They had to be granted citizenship of their homelands. They had to earn it.

A natural result of this stratification of class was that those non-Greeks who wanted to be upwardly mobile had to take on Greek ways. They had to dress Greek, be educated Greek and do Greek things. This isn't entirely unusual. Look at a picture of a

Japanese businessman. Notice him wearing a Kimono with multiple layers that color coordinate? Notice how his long hair is shaved in the front and gathered into a topknot at the back? No? No, he has a western style haircut and wears a business suit. That is what businesspeople all around the world wear. Cultures borrow from each other constantly.

Roman Culture

From the beginning of the Republic, and stretching back into the period of monarchy, Rome had a societal arrangement we call the client patron system. Understanding how things went down in Rome gets a lot easier to understand when you know about this.

The first thing to understand is that in Rome, there were two sorts of Roman citizens. The patricians were wealthy landowners who were able to afford to be educated. The plebeians were the working class, whether farmers or merchants, who did not have the leisure time to devote to education. Life for these two sorts of people was very different. It turned out that there were things these two sorts of people could do for each other.

Plebeians lived life close to financial ruin. One robbery or bad harvest and they could find themselves in deep trouble. Having a patrician as a patron was like having a rich uncle that could, if needed, take care of you during hard times. Patrons could be called on at need to give their clients food or money. Because they were educated, patrons would give legal advice, explain laws, and even represent their clients legally. With a patron around, there was a safety net around the edges of life.

Having clients lent patrons prestige. Clients would follow their patron around, which showed the munificence[1] of their patron.

---

1. Quality of being great in generosity.

When the patron spoke in public, his clients were a mob of support to cheer and applaud whenever he made a point. While the financial thing normally went the other way, in extreme cases a patron could draw on the resources of his clients.

Really important men could have other patricians as clients. Eventually this formed a sort of web to Roman society that stretched up to powerful senators and the emperor. The relationship between Herod and Pompey, and later Antony and Augustus, was of this sort. Herod was a client king, owing his loyalty to his benefactor and patron in Roman government.

A last patron client relationship was that of slave owner and recently freed slave. The freedman would be granted Roman citizenship and was expected to become a client of his former master or of his family. This brings us to the topic of citizenship.

Whether you were a patrician or plebeian, Roman citizenship was initially restricted to those who lived in Rome. As the nation grew, pressure from the other Latins mounted to give citizenship to them as well. When the rest of Italy was included, the groundwork for an enduring empire was laid. During the time of the Bible, this citizenship was restricted to a privileged few outside of the Italian peninsula.

Roman citizenship was the difference between being a ruler and being ruled by outsiders. Other than being born in Italy, citizenship could be acquired by being born in a Roman city outside of Italy, such as Corinth or Philippi. One could also serve in the military as an auxiliary for twenty-five years. The emperor could hand out citizenship by decree, which is where most of those Roman cities outside of Italy got theirs.

Citizenship conferred basic civic rights as you might expect. You could vote in assembly or run for office only if you were a citizen. Access to the court system was another benefit. You could have a legal contract or marriage which was upheld by Roman law.

It allowed you to sue someone in Roman court. It also entitled you to a trial in court, in Rome if requested, before facing legal sanctions.

Just to be clear, this meant that those who were not Roman citizens could be punished by the law without trial. It was perfectly alright to torture or even kill a non-Roman entirely without trial. A Roman citizen was also protected from the worst sorts of execution, such as crucifixion, no matter the crime. There were also taxes that applied only to those who lacked citizenship, like the one imposed on the Jews that Jesus addressed in Matthew chapter seventeen. There were laws of the same nature that applied only to conquered people. The law that non-Romans could be forced to carry a legionnaire's armor for a mile was an example of such a law.

On the subject of crucifixion, there are records of this form of execution going back to the Fifth Century BC in the Greek world, so it was not exclusively a Roman thing. This punishment could include the traditional cross that you are likely familiar with or the victim could be suspended from a post without a crossbar. The term could even refer to people who were impaled on a stake.

Today, Christians run around with cross necklaces and earrings. The symbol has lost most of its shock value. A cross was a method of execution and one of the nastiest ones available. Men would hang naked for days slowly dying. They would be set up in public places so their deaths could be used as a deterrent to others. We really don't kill people in anywhere as cruel a way anymore. When you read about "the cross" in the Bible, it might help to get the feeling to think of the electric chair, the gas chamber or perhaps a syringe full of lethal injection. "If anyone would come after me, let him deny himself and take up his *gas chamber* daily and follow me.[2]"

---

2. Luke 9:23

15

ISRAEL HAS IT UP TO ITS TONSILS WITH GREEK LEADERSHIP

And the goat is the king of Greece. And the great horn between his eyes is the first king. As for the horn that was broken, in place of which four others arose, four kingdoms shall arise from his nation, but not with his power.

Judea during the Persian and early Hellenistic periods was ruled by the High Priest. He had both the religious authority and the day-to-day temporal authority. This is why it was the High Priest who decided to not send Alexander aid when he sent a messenger. It was also the High Priest who went out to meet him when he approached. Jerusalem was like a Temple with a city attached. It should come as no surprise then that religious observance was very important to Jews both living in Jerusalem and scattered throughout the empire. They remained separate as a people through those observances. They were not to be like the nations around them.

That was the plan at least. The fact was that after the

Hellenistic takeover, the rich merchants and leaders increasingly took on Greek ways for that upward social mobility. By leaders, I mean priests. The large proportion of the priests taking on Greek ways was going to be an issue.

The High Priest was named Alexander, and he was a Hellenist. He desired that the Jews be free to Hellenize as much as they liked. He requested, and received, a Gymnasium. In case you aren't familiar with a Greek Gymnasium, it was where men went to exercise naked. They also often had baths. The Hellenizing Jewish boys were ashamed of, and tried to hide, their circumcisions. Alexander also permitted idols to be placed within the Temple grounds. For Jews who wanted to remain faithful to God, this was not the sort of behavior one wanted from one's High Priest.

The Seleucid king of Syria, Antiochus IV, called himself "Epiphanes" or "comes from god" but he was known on the sly as "Epimanes," or "the mad." Antiochus had meddled in the selection of the high priesthood. He had replaced Alexander with Menelaus. Menelaus was even more of a Hellenizer than Alexander.

Antiochus had been about to take Alexandria and conquer Egypt at last when he was met outside the city by Roman general Gaius Popilius Laenas. Laenas informed Antiochus that the Roman senate had debated the issue, held a vote and had decided that he was not conquering Egypt. Antiochus asked for a day to think it over. Laenas responded by drawing a circle around him in the sand and telling him he needed to decide before he stepped out.

By this point, there was no longer any debate about who wore the pants[1] in the Mediterranean. Antiochus had his choice of defiance, which would mean the likely end of the Seleucid Empire

---

1. Or in the case of the Romans, the togas.

and almost certainly his cushy job as emperor or he could be humiliated in front of all of his men by obeying.

After his disastrous humiliation at the hands of the Romans, Antiochus IV returned to find that Alexander had taken back his place as High Priest from Menelaus. It didn't come at a good time for him. He flew off the handle a hair. If he couldn't say boo to Rome, he could still take out his frustrations on those stubborn Jews.

At the command of Antiochus IV, the Mad, troops entered Jerusalem and began looting the city and killing the population. He entered the Temple and sacrificed a pig on the altar of God, consecrating it instead to Zeus. He made a decree that altars be set up throughout Judea and the priests be made to sacrifice swine on them to Zeus as well. Priests were also to be forced to eat of the swine once sacrificed. No longer were Jewish children to be circumcised. Hellenization was no longer optional. With that he ordered the building of a citadel overlooking the Temple and departed with ten thousand Jewish slaves.

The Samaritans had their own temple on Mount Gerizim. Unlike when they told Alexander the Great that they were Jews too and should be afforded the same tax exemptions as the ones in Jerusalem, this time they said they were Sidonians. "No need to come up here and murder everyone Mr. the Mad, we will just change the name of our temple to the Temple of Jupiter Hellinus." With that the Samaritans were square with Antiochus.

The Jews were having a harder time of it. Antiochus had men roaming the countryside forcing swine sacrifices and inspecting baby boys for signs of circumcision. Antiochus had a one strike program. Disobedience meant death. Women who circumcised their sons anyhow were crucified with their babies' bodies hung around their necks. Priests who refused to sacrifice pigs to Zeus were killed until someone did the sacrifice. Then all the priests gathered round the table for a dinner of ham. Anyone who didn't eat up was sent to his tomb without dinner.

The Maccabean Revolution

When we join the generation of Jews who walked the earth with Christ, independence will be a living memory. As Rome applied the boot as conquerors, the Jews would not think of themselves as a people who had been subject to others since the fall of the Southern kingdom. They would have the raw hatred of being a conquered people who were until recently free. They would also have messianic expectations. The road to freedom often begins with violence. This particular spot of violence was known as the Maccabean revolution.

One day the swine sacrifice task force visited the town of Modiin. There they ordered the respected priest Mattathias to perform the pig sacrifice. Mattathias was a good choice in the sense that having five grown sons made him a well-respected figure in town. When he refused, a Hellenized Jew stepped forward to do the ritual. Mattathias was not a great choice in the sense that he had five grown sons that would rather be dead than apostatize. It was then that Mattathias and those five grown sons pulled out swords and began getting to work. First, they killed the priest before he could do an abomination. Then they worked the Seleucid official over somewhat with their swords. Then the outlaw Jewish priests fled into the wilderness with other Jews who preferred death to apostasy. This, if you can believe it, was the birth of what would become the sect of the Pharisees.

Now you might think that the rebels would begin to strike imperial Seleucid targets but that is where you would be mistaken. This war was primarily about removing the abomination from Judah. The rebels began hitting communities of Hellenized Jews. Their primary targets were law breakers. Now it was fatal to eat pork and also fatal to not eat pork, depending on who was in town. While they were in town they circumcised any little boys that had not yet gotten that done.

Now don't hear me saying they didn't fight the Seleucids; they made circumcision policeman skyrocket up the list of most dangerous jobs. It wasn't long before you couldn't find anyone who was willing to roam the land forcing priests to eat bacon. The rebellion was on.

After a year of this sort of thing Mattathias died. He told his adult sons that Judas was in charge of the rebellion. Judas' nickname was Maccabeus, or "The Hammer[2]". The revolution got its name from him.

The Samaritans decided to do the Empire a favor and put down the rebellion. However, their force did not meet with universal success[3]. Next, a Syrian general brought his army to deal with the threat. He augmented his army with volunteers from the Hellenized Jews. Although he had numerical superiority, he also did not meet with success[4]. Whether this was because God was on Judas' side or because phalanx warfare was ill suited to the hilly terrain, I will leave for you to decide. Either way, Judas used hit and run tactics to break the invaders' morale. The rebels had won again.

All of this success brought ever growing fame to the Maccabean revolt. This resulted in a marked increase of warriors who were willing to fight for Judas. The situation was getting out of hand pretty quickly. The emperor needed to do something about it if order was to be maintained.

---

2. Or in French, Martel.
3. They got butchered.
4. Butchered.

Antiochus himself was indisposed. He had to go on campaign into Persia where the Parthians threatened his eastern border, as if having the Romans to his west wasn't bad enough. He left Lycius in charge of his affairs in the region. He expected to see that Jerusalem was burned to the ground and all of the Jews enslaved when he came back, and he expected his son to be safe.

Lycius ordered a general to take an enormous army down to Judea and see about killing off Judas and his rebels as a first step. When they arrived, they sent out an advance party to fall on Judas' camp by night. Judas saw them coming and slipped around them as they came. He then fell on the Seleucid camp, and scattered the troops with a surprise attack. As they looted and killed, the advance force found the rebel camp abandoned. As the Seleucid army returned, they saw their own camp ablaze. Morale got a little low, and they decided to leave.

All of this defeating much larger forces was having the most salubrious[5] effect on Judas' reputation. God-fearing Jews were flocking to his banner. Enemy troops were hesitant to give battle. It only became more so when another Seleucid force, this one even larger, was routed the following year. Lycius was forced to go recruiting so he could get an army large enough to deal with this rebellion which had gotten more than just a little out of hand.

The Maccabeans took this pause in the action to enter Jerusalem. The High Priest would have dearly loved to keep them out, but the city walls had been torn down by Antiochus. Three years after Antiochus' reign of terror, Judas presided over the cleansing of the Temple in Jerusalem. It is from this time that we get the Feast of Lights holiday, also known as Hanukkah.

There was still a war going on. On the military side, Judas fortified Jerusalem once more. After that he went on the offensive.

---

5. Health-giving.

He struck the Edomites, killing a large number and looting. He also razed the Ammonite city of Jazer, looting it and leading away the women and children as slaves. Why did he do that? It was what Judah did before it became a province in an empire. The boot of the Empire was off, and the Jews went back to attacking their old enemies. It was just like old times.

Fair is fair, and their neighbors decided that they could attack back. Judas faced two invasions simultaneously, one at Gilead and one from the north in Galilee. He split his now considerable army. Simon led the smaller force to face the smaller invasion in Galilee while Judas led his host to face the other threat. Both forces were successful. Judas' battle was mostly the enemy fleeing at the sight of his approach. On his return Judas destroyed several cities, killing the lawbreakers and foreigners he found.

Antiochus the Mad just couldn't catch a break. What he could catch was a fatal illness while campaigning, unsuccessfully I might add, against Parthia. On learning this, Lycius named Antiochus' nine-year-old son Antiochus V. With the succession settled, Lycius took his overwhelming army down to deal with this Judas Maccabeus.

The problem with a reputation is that a fellow can get to believing it. When Judas saw the overwhelmingly large army complete with phalanx troops and elephants, he decided to try fighting straight up instead of doing the old hit and run. This did not go as he might have hoped[6]. Judas' brother Eliezer tried to turn the tide of battle by charging an elephant and stabbing it, but this just got him killed[7]. Judas retreated behind his new walls at Jerusalem.

The siege went long, and Judas' supplies were running out.

---

6. Double Butchered.
7. It fell on him. And then there were four.

Fortunately for him, Lycius got word that some people were trying to take the regency over the boy emperor. He needed to get back to court at Antioch to deal with that. What was more, he would need his overwhelmingly large army on hand to deal with any backchat. Lycius offered Judas a deal. The Jews may live by their law and have peace. Judas agreed, but Lycius did execute the High Priest and replaced him with Alcimus. Lycius then went home to deal with matters.

The problem with these royal families was that they just did not get along. Take the case of this guy Demetrius. Demetrius was living in Rome as a hostage to ensure the good behavior of his father, Emperor Seleucius IV. While he was there, his father was murdered by a usurper. Not to worry though, his uncle Antiochus avenged his father by killing that rotten usurper. Unfortunately, Uncle Antiochus crowned himself Antiochus IV, usurping Demetrius' throne and eventually leaving it to Lycius on behalf of Antiochus V.

This same Demetrius, despite not having one of the two approved names for a Seleucid emperor, took over the empire from Lycius and his little cousin[8]. Alcimus, the new High Priest, dropped by to complain about Judas. Demetrius agreed that Judas needed to be dealt with, so he sent an army under the command of Nicanor to accomplish the job.

Judas lost his second battle against Nicanor and was forced to retreat to the citadel that Antiochus had built to oppress Judah. Nicanor told the people of Jerusalem that they needed to hand over Judas or he was going to burn down their Temple. This caused Judas to emerge and face Nicanor in the field again. This time Judas won through the brilliant strategy of charging up and killing Nicanor personally.

---

8. Of course he killed them, don't be silly.

The Seleucid army gone for the moment, Judas returned to Jerusalem. There he found Alcimus the High Priest, who suddenly was stricken of God and died[9]. The people of Judah decided that Judas should be the new High Priest. His first act as High Priest was to send word to Rome that he wanted to be its friend. Rome agreed and the Senate ratified a league between Rome and Judah.

Demetrius, ignoring the league, sent another leader, Bacchides, with a sizeable army to dry gulch Judah. He found Judas himself encamped and came upon him by surprise. The Judeans panicked and fled, leaving Judas with less than a thousand to face over twenty thousand. Sometimes when you have too big a reputation, you can't let it down by running away[10]. Judas went down in a blaze of glory, surrounded by his enemies[11]. The remaining brothers fled to the wilderness with Bacchides hot on their heels. They are forced to swim the Jordan to escape from the heavily armored Greek hoplites.

What saved the Hasmonean[12] bacon[13] was that Alexander Balas, claiming to be the son of Antiochus IV, arrived at the city of Ptolemais. He had an army of mercenaries and the backing of the Roman Senate[14]. He set himself up as a rival emperor to Demetrius[15]. Both of them needed to gather as much support as they could for the inevitable conflict.

Demetrius wrote to Judas' surviving brother Jonathan asking that they let bygones be bygones. He informed him that he had

---

9. According to Josephus. Stricken by Judas seems more likely.
10. Not counting the first two times he was forced to flee.
11. And then there were three.
12. The family name of Judas and his brothers.
13. Not that they would ever eat bacon. They would likely kill you for offering it to them.
14. Rome liked to keep the Seleucids weak by introducing occasional contenders for the throne.
15. This is getting out of hand, now there are two of them.

released all of the Jewish prisoners. Demetrius invited Jonathan to rule in Jerusalem and raise an army for its defense.

Alexander, not to be outdone, sent Jonathan a crown and purple robe and appointed him High Priest of Israel. Alexander knew that it was men working for Demetrius that had killed Jonathan's brother and sent armies against Jerusalem. Jonathan was in the bag to help him.

Demetrius knew these things too. He wrote a second time commending Jonathan for his loyalty and not joining that stinker Alexander. As a royal reward for all of his loyalty, Demetrius would gladly give the Jews a number of tax exemptions, finance the sacrifices, hand over the citadel, and personally pay to have the Temple repaired.

The whole issue became academic when Alexander and Demetrius decided to settle the issue with their armies. Jonathan backed the winner and reaped the spoils of helping Alexander kill Demetrius.

Jonathan also reaped the spoils of Ashdod and the surrounding region before he burned the city and the temple to Dagon. He would have done the same to Ashkelon, but its rulers paid him off.

As a side note, one of the times Antiochus meddled with the High Priest office, he disinherited a man named Onias. Onias fled to Egypt where he convinced Ptolemy to allow him to build a temple there just like the one in Jerusalem, complete with Levites and Aaronic priests. He was inspired by Isaiah 19:19. Ironically, he had better claim to be High Priest than any of the Hasmonean High Priests since they were not of the line of Zadok.

16

HASMONEAN DYNASTY OF JUDAH

And as Jesus reclined at table in the house, behold, many tax collectors and sinners came and were reclining with Jesus and his disciples. And when the Pharisees saw this, they said to his disciples, "Why does your teacher eat with tax collectors and sinners?" But when he heard it, he said, "Those who are well have no need of a physician, but those who are sick. Go and learn what this means: 'I desire mercy, and not sacrifice.' For I came not to call the righteous, but sinners."

Jonathan's high priesthood was cut short when he was tricked into dismissing his army and then betrayed by Trypho, the regent of Demetrius II, the current Seleucid emperor. They thought that by taking Jonathan and his family hostage, they could control the Jews. The last of the brothers, Simon, was acclaimed High Priest in Jerusalem. Simon felt bad about attacking Trypho, forcing him to kill his brother and his family, but he did what he had to do.[1]

The problems the Seleucids were having from Rome, Parthia, and constant squabbling over the throne, left Judah and the area relatively free. Not only Judah, but the surrounding peoples were suddenly running their own business. Simon coined money, showing the level of freedom they had. He had that citadel Antiochus the Mad built overlooking the Temple torn down and the hill it sat on leveled to the ground. It took three years but now the Temple was the highest point in Jerusalem. He could do things like that because Judah was free of imperial rule.

The treaty with Rome was renewed under Simon in 139 BC. This new incarnation of Judah, with a new ruler and with newfound independence was eager to be counted as one of Rome's friends. It was at this time that Rome sent out instructions to five eastern kings in almost twenty cities that the Jews in their cities were not to be harmed.

Freedom from the Seleucid Empire did not mean total peace. Simon's rule came crashing down when his son-in-law murdered him. He tried to kill Simon's sons too, but he missed one, John Hyrcanus. Hyrcanus wasn't at the feast where the murdering took place. Hyrcanus took his father's place as High Priest and ruled the Jews with the backing of his party. They stood in opposition to foreign rule and influence and in favor of complete devotion to following God's Law. Nonetheless, Hyrcanus did a few things during his rule that cost him favor with this party.

When Antiochus VII came to Judah with an army to regain control, Hyrcanus was forced to endure a long and brutal siege. This siege was of the fighting rather than the waiting around sort of siege. Hyrcanus decided that he did not need to drain his food

---

1. Sometimes it works out to go last.

resources by feeding noncombatants. He expelled the residents of Jerusalem that could not fight, such as the aged, women and children. Antiochus did not let them pass through his siege lines. What ended up happening was they starved to death at the base of the walls.

When Antiochus VII attacked Judah and took cities including Joppa, John Hyrcanus appealed to Rome for aid. Rome responded with a strongly worded message to Antiochus to restore what he had taken and a promise to debate in the Senate what was to be done in regards to the Jewish question. Antiochus, for his part, ignored Rome and laid siege to, and subsequently took Jerusalem. Judah became a client kingdom to Syria once again. Judah was made to pay tribute, an indemnity, and the walls of Jerusalem were destroyed.

When Hyrcanus came to terms with Antiochus, those terms included him breaking into David's tomb to get gold and silver to pay Antiochus off. He also had to ride with Antiochus to help him fight in Parthia. Most of his native Jewish fighters had perished in the siege. That was fine since he had more of that tomb of David money, so he hired mercenaries. Independence was over briefly.

After the death of Antiochus, Hyrcanus returned with his army. It was experienced and hardened by battle. He decided to use it against the Samaritans. He laid siege to their city. The Seleucids tried to interfere, but were useless. After a year, Hyrcanus took Samaria, burning it to the ground. He enslaved the population and led it off. He also took Shechem and Mount Gerizim. After taking Gerizim, he burned the temple there to the ground. Barely pausing, Hyrcanus turned against the Idumeans[2]. He conquered their cities. They were permitted to either leave or convert to Judaism.

---

2. By this time the Edomites were called Idumeans.

By the time of Hyrcanus, the party of traditionalism that supported the Hasmoneans had taken the name Pharisees. This party had the ear of the people. If they spoke ill of the High Priest, people believed it. They had occasion to do so often in the past before the rise of the Hasmonean High Priests. Most of those had been Hellenizers of the first water. The Pharisees saw themselves as the repository of the traditions of the fathers that had to be kept along with the Law of Moses. The opposition to them came from the rich priests, now called Sadducees, who maintained that keeping the Law of Moses was sufficient. The independence of Israel had brought the debate over a bit from when they had been subjects of the Seleucids. Nobody was openly advocating for Gymnasium or ditching the dietary rules anymore.

I bring this up because, prior to his death, Hyrcanus switched from Pharisee to Sadducee. He left his throne to his oldest son, Aristobulus. The reason for the switch quickly became apparent. Aristobulus I put a crown on his own head and declared that he was king of Israel. The Pharisees exploded in outrage. He was High Priest without being of the line of Zadok and King but not of the line of David.

Had I been there I would have been outraged by him throwing his mother and all but one of his brothers into the dungeon. His mother died of starvation in a cell for the crime of disagreeing with her son on how the kingdom was to be run. The one brother he did allow out, he was tricked into murdering. This trick was played on him by his wife, Salome Alexandria.

Aristobulus I only reigned briefly but had a number of conquests. He expanded the kingdom into the north into the region of Galilee. Once again, the inhabitants were given to option of converting or leaving.

Guilt from murdering his brother caused Aristobulus' health to decline rapidly. After his death his surviving brothers were released from prison. Alexander Jannaeus took up where his older brother left off as king of Israel. The Pharisees were kept off of the boil because the wife of Aristobulus, Salome Alexandria, was a Pharisee. Alexander Jannaeus also took up where his brother left off by marrying her[3].

Alexander Jannaeus started his military career by getting involved in an internal Ptolemaic dispute when it spilled over into Syria. He got his army beaten up to no small extent and his countryside ransacked. He went on to take Gaza and Gadara, which annoyed the Nabataean Arabs so much that they invaded and funded rebellions among the dissatisfied Pharisees in the countryside.

These rebellions at home were no small deal. He spent a great deal of time fighting with his own people. He even got pelted with fruit when he didn't do a ceremony correctly. The people of Jerusalem cried out vile slurs against his ancestry. Things escalated until the rebels enlisted Seleucid aid in crushing his army. It turns out that having the Pharisees against you can mean a heap of trouble.

Things between Alexander and the Pharisees got so bad that he took out his ire on them by crucifying eight hundred Pharisees. As if this was not brutal enough, he had their wives and children brought before them as they died and murdered them.

When you read your New Testament accounts, one of the miracles you did not know you were reading about was the miracle of the Sadducees and the Pharisees agreeing about anything. This act by Alexander Jannaeus on behalf of the Sadducees was going to set the tone between the two groups. It was bad blood of the worst sort.

Alexander Jannaeus eventually got the Nabataeans off of his

---

3. Deuteronomy 25:5

back by giving them what they wanted, some land. The rebel faction collapsed, and he was able to go on a spree of conquest, expanding his rule and forcing the conquered to convert.

When he died, Salome Alexandria purchased peace with the Pharisees by handing over Alexander Jannaeus' body to them. In doing so, the new administration was in the camp of the Pharisees.

Alexander Jannaeus' son Hyrcanus was made High Priest but he did not rule. While Salome Alexandria reigned as queen, the Pharisees ran the kingdom. They formed the Sanhedrin and took over much of the power of government, including serving as the Supreme Court. They quickly began taking revenge by executing Jannaeus' Sadducee advisors. This annoyed the other son, Aristobulus II, who began taking fortresses throughout Judea in preparation to declaring himself king. It would be a contested succession; Hyrcanus II verses Aristobulus II.

17

ROMAN CONQUEST OF JUDEA

> *Then Herod, when he saw that he had been tricked by the wise men, became furious, and he sent and killed all the male children in Bethlehem and in all that region who were two years old or under, according to the time that he had ascertained from the wise men.*

When prophecy returned in preparation for the coming of Christ, the region of Judea was a very different place from what it was at the close of the Old Testament. Israel had a king, but that king was an official beholden to the Roman Empire. The time has come to see how Rome came to rule the area and how Herod the Great came to be the king of Judea.

Rome was a settlement of Latins on the banks of the Tiber River that enjoyed the revenue of the trade between the Greek cities to their south and the Etruscans to their north. Most of their culture, with the exception of their government, was borrowed from one or the other of these two[1]. Their chief god was Jupiter.

About the time king Uzziah was fortifying Judah, Rome was founded under the rule of kings about 753 BC. When one of their kings was involved in the rape of a chaste woman, the Romans overthrew the monarchy in 503 BC, about the time Cyrus was letting Judah return to its land. They developed in its stead a new government where the people ruled, if those people came from one of the ruling or patristic families. From these families three hundred Senators formed a ruling council. The offices of chief executive[2] and judicial head[3] were filled by two Consuls who served for one year each. These Consuls were picked from the patricians. During times of emergency, the Senate could vest supreme power in the hands of a single dictator.

The rest of the people were called the plebeians. They did not get any say in government initially. They did make up most of the soldiers in the army. When enemies would menace, they would commonly bargain for civil rights in return for fighting. Eventually, they got an official called the Tribune. This guy could veto anything the Consuls did.

From 390-280 BC, Rome waged war with other people in Italy to take control. Once they defeated the other Latins, they allied with them. Later these other Latins were given citizenship, and Rome's powerbase was a territorial state rather than just a city.

Rome did not finish with war after unifying Italy. When they got to the sea, the Romans decided to fight the Phoenicians for Sicily, Sardinia, and Corsica. Somewhere along the way, they got embroiled in the fighting among the Greek successor states as

---

1. It is hard to tell because the Etruscans were also heavily influenced by the Greeks.
2. President or king.
3. Judge.

well. In 146 BC Rome destroyed both Carthage and Corinth. It had conquered both its Phoenician and Greek enemies.

This led to some internal problems at home. The Roman army, at its core, was made up of small-holding farmers who put on armor, went to war to defend Rome, and then returned home. They then would remove their armor and go back to being farmers. That was how it was supposed to work. Unfortunately, because of all the war, and frankly all of the victory, this system broke down.

The small-holding farmers were unable to work their lands because of the constant war. It was hard to get a crop in when you spent the whole year in foreign lands cutting their soldiers down. The land was bought up and made into plantations. There were slaves galore from all of the conquest, so labor was not a problem. The dispossessed soldiers moved to Rome where they formed an unruly underclass that might riot at a moments' notice.

Generals took to forming their own armies that were loyal to their generals, not Rome. These legions were paid in money or land once their service was over. A prime example of this sort of army was the one belonging to Julius Caesar. He published accounts of his wars to let the people of Rome know how he was conquering Gaul, modern day France.

Another such general was Pompey. Rome was in the process of absorbing Syria in an effort to spread the Roman peace[4]. Pompey had defeated Mithridates of Pontus and Tigranes of Armenia. This left a vacuum of power that Rome had to fill to avoid disorder in the region. An independent Judean state was no longer in the best interests of Rome as it had been when it was providing a distraction to Syria. At this time unrest was brewing in Judah between the parties of the Pharisees and the Sadducees. In addition to this

---

4. Peace, Rome's favorite reason for war.

struggle, the high priesthood was in dispute between Hyrcanus II and his brother Aristobulus II. This disorder was a threat to the Roman peace in the region and an excellent pretext for Roman interference.

The dispute in question was all the more damaging to the regional peace because Hyrcanus had enlisted the aid of the Nabataean Arab troops to help him regain his throne. When I say Hyrcanus, I of course mean Antipater, his advisor. Hyrcanus did not have the proper drive to betray his family and to see them dead if it was necessary to hold to his power as king. His counselor, Antipater the Idumean, possessed this drive in abundance. After Hyrcanus had lost the battle with Aristobulus, he had agreed to acknowledge his brother's right to rule. In return, Hyrcanus was allowed to live. Antipater convinced him to get the backing of the Nabataean Arab forces in return for giving back land once he was king again. This Antipater was the father of Herod the Great. He had connections among the Nabataeans and desired to rule Judea from behind the placid Hyrcanus. Aristobulus proved no match for the Nabataeans and was forced to take refuge in the Temple.

Pompey responded by sending Roman forces into Judea in 65 BC to keep disorder from breaking out. Both Aristobulus and Hyrcanus sent petitions and bribes to Pompey's legate. He decided to solve the issue by threatening to attack the Nabataeans, which dissolved the forces Hyrcanus was depending on to enforce his claims against Aristobulus. Later both brothers appealed directly to Pompey who reserved judgment in the matter. Both of the brothers put themselves in a subservient position to Rome by appealing to Roman judgment in the matter of who would rule. Judah's independence as a nation was coming to an end.

Pompey continued in the region, fighting the Nabataeans. Aristobulus decided to hedge his bets against Rome choosing his brother by entrenching himself in the fortress of Alexandrion.

Pompey responded to this defiance by marching on Judah. Aristobulus fled to Jerusalem and prepared for attack. When he saw Roman troops, Aristobulus went to Pompey to sue for peace. Aristobulus agreed to pay an indemnity and accept a Roman garrison in Jerusalem. Aristobulus' supporters, however, refused to admit the occupying army. Aristobulus was arrested, and Jerusalem was besieged by Rome. Aristobulus' followers knew they couldn't hold the whole city so they holed up in the Temple enclosure. Hyrcanus' men allowed Rome into the city but the taking of the Temple enclosure took three months. Once the Romans broke through, they murdered priests, and Pompey himself entered the Holy of Holies.

In the aftermath of the conquest, Rome had the walls of the city razed along with those of the Temple complex. Garrisons of Roman soldiers were left. Judah was put under tribute, and taxes were collected throughout Judea. Much of the territory taken by Judah under the Hasmonean kings was taken away and either given independence under Rome or absorbed into Syria. Thousands of Jews, loyal to Aristobulus, were deported in slave's shackles to Rome.

Judah, even so, was not absorbed into the Roman Empire. Hyrcanus was left as the client ruler. Pompey's actions were to weaken Judah so that it could not prove to be a threat to Roman interests in the region, while preserving Jewish pride by leaving them a native ruler and so forestall rebellion. The independence of Judah was gone in all but name.

For better or worse, Aristobulus' faction now contended against Rome for Judean independence. Rome chose Hyrcanus. If the Aristobulus faction were to rule, it had to do it over Rome's objection. Alexander, Aristobulus' elder son, escaped from Roman custody and raised a rebellion against Rome in 57 BC. He overran Hyrcanus' forces and occupied the main fortresses in the area. It required Roman forces to step in, and Alexander was dislodged only with difficulty.

Aristobulus and his younger son Antigonus escaped from Roman custody and in 56 BC they raised an army and fought against the Roman occupation. They were badly beaten and, unable to defend Machaeros, they were captured and returned to Rome. Alexander resurfaced and renewed the revolution. He marched through Galilee and Samaria, killing some Romans and besieging others on Mt. Gerizim. The return of Roman forces quickly scattered the rebels.

After Pompey conquered Syria and Judea for the glory of Rome, Caesar defied the Senate by failing to disband his army as he approached Rome. It was on between these two generals with control of all Rome in the balance.

Hyrcanus and Antipater switched sides from Pompey to Caesar. Pompey fled to Egypt where he was assassinated. There was a conflict between Cleopatra and her brother over the rule of Egypt. Since Caesar had chased Pompey there he became enmeshed in that conflict. While Hyrcanus lent aid like a good subject, Antipater led troops. It was on this campaign that he distinguished himself in battle. The commander of the other half of the army broke and it would have been a slaughter, but Antipater finished his part on the battlefield and rescued his comrade. Caesar recognized his contribution by giving him Roman citizenship and extending to him his official friendship.

The wars between Pompey and Caesar brought about the deaths of Aristobulus and Alexander, ironically in Caesar's service. They also saw Hyrcanus receive more autonomy in return for his aid to Caesar. Hyrcanus renewed the treaty of friendship with Rome and received permission to refortify Jerusalem. Antipater was made governor of Judea, but his power was limited because of the return of much of the authority to Hyrcanus. This mattered less than it might since Hyrcanus was in the habit of letting Antipater do as he liked.

Antipater did get his sons installed as governors. Judea was under the administration of Phasael, his older son, and Galilee in the north was under Herod, only fifteen at the time. The rebellion of Alexander had not died, and it took the form of anti-Roman brigands who struck from Galilee at the Syrian Decapolis. Herod had paid for the privilege of leading the Roman army of coastal Syria. He showed his mettle by breaking up the brigands and executing their leader, Ezechias.

The Pharisees did not appreciate the fact that he killed the bandits without having them lawfully tried by the Sanhedrin. This concern for the law was but a mask for their support for the anti-Roman faction. It was not lost to them that the Roman governors who wielded the power in Judea were Idumeans. They badgered Hyrcanus to make Herod appear before the Sanhedrin. They had planned on condemning him, but Herod decided not to show for the last day of trial so he wasn't around for sentencing. Later, when the government was in his hands, Herod executed almost all of the members of that Sanhedrin.

The dispersed Jews in almost every place but Babylon were under the rule now of Rome. Because the Jewish faith was viewed as non-revolutionary towards Rome at the time and held to high moral standards, it was respected and permitted to go on. The privileges that Jews had in the empire to practice their faith freely were codified into law by Julius Caesar. He exempted synagogues from his closure order and granted them rights. The Jews were permitted to assemble for religious purposes and hold common meals. They were allowed to gather for Sabbaths and to observe festivals and holy days. They were exempted from military service, and it was not permitted to force them to appear in court on a

Sabbath. Jews in the Roman Empire were free to follow the Law of Moses.

The Temple tax was another example of Jews being supported in Rome. Jews were allowed to collect Temple tax and hold it in the synagogue. The tax and its carriers were inviolate while they were taking the tax to Jerusalem. Theft of the tax or of a roll of the Scriptures was illegal and punishable as sacrilege.

These privileges continued after the death of Caesar and were reaffirmed under Augustus. Augustus even decreed that if the corn[5] dole was given out on the Sabbath, the Jews' portion should be reserved to be doled out after the Sabbath. In many ways Roman rule was beneficial to their Jewish subjects in ways that went beyond the peace that Rome brought.

While Caesar was in the area doing Pompey down, he stopped by Egypt where he paid a visit to Cleopatra. Okay, what happened was Caesar was in the area and Cleopatra was in a dispute with her brother over control of Egypt. She had herself brought to Caesar draped in sheets. Cleopatra got what she wanted, to rule Egypt and they made an alliance between Rome and Egypt as well as a little boy.

The Caesars[6] returned to Rome where Caesar took upon himself the titles of Dictator, Tribune, and Consul all at once. The Senate decided that Caesar was a little too much like a king for their taste and murdered him.

The two main murderers took off to the east. Brutus took over as governor of Greece. Cassius took over in Syria. The Senate awarded the navy to Pompey's son Pompey Sixtus. Sixtus held

---

5. Generic name for grain. What we call corn was unknown in Ancient Rome, being endemic to the Americas.
6. Okay, technically they were not married.

himself aloof from the upcoming struggles, safe behind his navy in Sicily.

Meanwhile Antony and Octavian were piping hot about the murder. Octavian received Caesar's money and right to call himself Caesar. Once he used the money he inherited to pay the legions, he also inherited Caesar's armies. Antony and Octavian formed a triumvirate with another guy who did not matter in the least little bit[7].

In order to both cement power and fund their upcoming war, Antony and Octavian published an enemies list. Everyone on the list was slaughtered and their property taken to fund the war. A full third of the Senate were on that list. After the gaps were filled with Octavian's nominees, the Senate was much more favorable to him.

With money for their war, Antony and Octavian met Cassius and Brutus at Philippi[8]. After this, Octavian ruled in the west and Antony in the east. Now Marc Antony was the most powerful individual in the Judean region. He took up with Cleopatra of Egypt, who had been with Julius Caesar before his death. Herod sent gifts to Antony and in return was made Tetrarch along with his older brother Phasael.

Roman rule in the region was not entirely uninterrupted. The Parthian Empire was spreading west. When opposing Rome, it could help if there was a power to challenge them. Antigonus, son of Aristobulus, retook Jerusalem with the aid of the Parthian Empire. Herod managed to escape through Egypt to Rome. His brother Phasael was not so lucky.

Once in power, Antigonus took the high priesthood from his

---

7. It doesn't matter what his name is, don't bother. Okay, fine. Lepidus. Go ahead, look him up. You'll be bored.
8. Of course they killed them.

Uncle Hyrcanus. He had his uncle maimed so he could no longer fulfill the role of High Priest. The Parthians then deported Hyrcanus to Babylon where he was treated with respect and admiration.

In Rome, Antony and Octavian Caesar both spoke for Herod before the Senate. It was decided that Herod should be the king of Judea. Rome was not overly worried about the fact that Herod was not of the royal blood. They didn't even seem to care that he wasn't, strictly speaking, Jewish. His family had been Idumeans forced to convert under the conquests of John Hyrcanus.

With the assurances of Rome in his pocket and a Roman army at his back, Herod returned to Judea to take his kingdom from the Hasmonean ruler, Antigonus. After taking Joppa, he moved against the Judeans in the countryside. He also was compelled to rescue his family who were holding out in the Masada. The Masada was a fortress on top of a sheer mesa in the Judean wilderness. It was, bar none, the hardest egg to crack in the whole land. Later it would hold out against Rome for years after the fall of Jerusalem.

After years of fighting, Herod laid siege to Jerusalem itself with an army made up of both Roman and Jewish warriors. This siege lasted five months and necessitated breaking through the walls Caesar had allowed built. It ended with looting by the Roman soldiers, slaughter of the inhabitants, and Herod as king. In doing so he subjugated Judah to Rome and acknowledged Rome's right to rule over them.

Now Rome had a client king who could be counted on to value the interests of Rome as his own. Herod could not rule without Roman backing and accepting his crown from the hands of Rome acknowledged the submission of Judah. Herod's submission was put to the test when Antony, after marrying Cleopatra, gave portions of Herod's kingdom to her as a gift. She received the lucrative port cities on the Levant coast that had been Herod's as well as balsam and palm groves around Jericho. This gift showed that Roman leaders, even friends of Herod's like Antony, continued to treat Judah as property of Rome as opposed to an ally or friend.

Herod's relationship with Hyrcanus was complicated. His father had run Judea in Hyrcanus' name. Now Herod was king and Hyrcanus had returned from exile in Babylon. Herod married Mariamne who was a granddaughter of both Aristobulus II and Hyrcanus II, cementing his claim through marriage as best he could.

Immediately after defeating the murderers, Octavian and Antony started giving each other side eye. Someone was going to rule Rome. Octavian got to work making sure that would be him. Marcus Agrippa, one of Octavian's trusted lieutenants, decided to do something about the fleet inequalities. Rome had a fleet superior to Egypt's, but it was in the hands of Sixtus. Sixtus wasn't about to give the heir of the man who killed his dad the fleet he needed to be emperor. Marcus Agrippa dug a lake to train his navy so Sixtus couldn't hinder him. Once trained, his new navy met and defeated Sixtus'.

Having a navy wasn't the only advantage Egypt had. It also had a queen who was notoriously friendly with Roman leaders. Antony divorced Octavian's sister to marry Cleopatra. He then drew up a will that left large swathes of his Roman territories to their mutual offspring.

The Roman navy trapped the Egyptian at Actium in Greece. Cleopatra and Antony chose to escape rather than die in glorious combat. It wasn't long before Octavian arrived in Egypt. Since Antony had abandoned his army, he was defenseless. Both Antony and Cleopatra decided on suicide.

Afterwards Rome lost its republic for good as Octavian

became the emperor, Augustus. The Romans didn't mind since a century of endless war had also gone with it. Augustus brought peace since nobody was foolhardy enough to fight with him.

Unfortunately, Herod was a close friend of Antony, and Antony was at war with Octavian. If you know anything about Augustus, being on his wrong side was to be on the wrong side of history. Herod feared that Augustus would replace him with Hyrcanus now that Antony was out of the picture. That was the problem with keeping the man who actually belonged on the throne around once you were king. Married to his granddaughter or not, Herod was forced to put him before the Sanhedrin on disputable charges.

After seeing to Hyrcanus' execution, Herod traveled to confront Augustus. He left most of his family at Masada. Mariamne and his other Hasmonean relatives[9] were left at another fortress. If it did not go well with him, the men in charge of the fortress were ordered to kill them. When Mariamne found out about those orders, it chilled the romance in their relationship to no small extent.

Herod removed his crown and requested an audience with Augustus. He admitted aiding Antony in their war. In fact, he felt guilty he had not been able to do more than send him food. Antony had been a good friend to him. Augustus restored Herod's crown and told him to be as good a friend to him now that the conflict was over.

Herod supplied the Roman army generously as it moved through the area Augustus had to march through to defeat Egypt. On the march back Herod was even more generous. His behavior earned him the friendship of Augustus. He exchanged gifts with Augustus and spent time hobnobbing with Augustus and Agrippa.

---

9. The family that ruled Judea before Herod Usurped the throne.

Augustus restored the lands that Antony had taken in return for Herod's continued loyal service, but when Herod broke the peace of Rome by going to war with the Nabataeans, Augustus officially withdrew his friendship. Augustus' treatment, ironically, showed more respect for Judah's place as a nation than did Antony's.

On his return to Judea, gloriously both king and in one piece, he went immediately to tell the wonderful news to Mariamne. Mariamne was less than enthusiastic. Her jailors had told all. She had convinced the official in charge that if Herod was taken out, he would profit greatly when she was lifted up by Rome.

Herod's orders to kill her were intended to protect the rest of his family from the kill order that would no doubt have come from her and her mother Alexandria if they took power. Herod was crazy in love with Mariamne. It really hurt him to have to kill her and her mother. Herod did not lack that drive to do what was necessary to maintain power. He took after his father in that.

He had sent his two sons by Mariamne, Alexander and Aristobulus, to Rome for education and to make Romans of them. When they returned, they were the heirs apparent to the throne of Judea. Why wouldn't they be? They were of the Hasmonean blood unlike all of the other sons of Herod. They were royalty. Unfortunately, they were also surly and made no secret of the fact that they were disgruntled about the rest of their family being executed.

Herod, in order to curb their arrogance, introduced his son Antipater. Antipater was older but his mother was decidedly less royal. Antipater had his grandfather's drive in spades and began slandering Alexander and Aristobulus to their mutual father. Eventually it paid off when Herod had them both executed. We will get to the rest of Antipater's "payoff" after we look at some of Herod's accomplishments in office.

Herod was known as Herod the Great. This was not so much a commentary on his personality or decency. It was about his able rule and accomplishments. We have looked at his rule, how he was able to take the kingdom from the Parthian Empire and keep it through the wars of both Roman triumvirates. His main accomplishments were in the area of building.

He built the city of Caesarea on the coast. He also built the city of Sebaste on the ruins of the old city of Samaria. He built a fortress there of the same name. In Jerusalem he constructed a fortress which he named the Antonia in honor of his old friend Antony. He improved the fortifications at Masada.

Herod perhaps a bit less popularly did some building that increased the Roman character of his domain. He built a theatre in Jerusalem and an amphitheater outside town on the plains. He instituted a game which was held once every five years in honor of Caesar. He also set up wrestling, chariot races and gladiatorial shows complete with wild beasts.

Most famously, Herod rebuilt the Temple from the ground up. It was far larger and grander than it had been. This would be the Temple where Jesus taught and drove out money changers. The place was a real treat for the eyes with carvings and gold inlay to spare.

Herod also built up a big family. Even his ability to kill sons could not keep up with his ability to put them out. He had nine wives, and he managed to not kill the majority of them. He had a son Herod Philip, by the daughter of the High Priest Simon, also named Mariamne oddly enough. He had Herod Antipas and Archelaus by Malthace of Samaria. He also had a wife named Cleopatra, but she was from Jerusalem, not Egypt. They had Herod and Philip. I apologize for the confusing manner in which Herod named his children. I only report it; I don't make it up.

The problem with kings having so many sons was that it turned the palace into a hive of scheming and intrigue. Herod was paranoid enough to sacrifice his wife Mariamne and her two sons to keep power. Much of the scheming against the sons was accomplished by Antipater. Once they were dead, he began scheming against Herod as well. Herod was apprised of this and tossed him in the dungeon to keep him out of trouble.

In his waning days, Herod was paring an apple when he decided to use the knife on himself. His attempt was stopped, but it created a racket. Antipater, in his cell, began telling the officer about his good fortune. Little did he know that Herod still lived and was not amused by his ghoulish glee. Antipater preceded his father to the grave by five days.

In the end, Archelaus inherited the crown from his father where he proved to be a weak and ineffectual ruler. Rome gave and they took away. In this case they turned Judea into a province. Herod Antipas [10]became Tetrarch of Galilee and Phillip[11] became a tetrarch of other areas northeast of the Sea of Galilee.

---

10. Son of Malthace the Samarian.
11. Son of Cleopatra of Jerusalem.

18

JESUS!

> *Long ago, at many times and in many ways, God spoke to our fathers by the prophets, but in these last days he has spoken to us by his Son, whom he appointed the heir of all things, through whom also he created the world. He is the radiance of the glory of God and the exact imprint of his nature*

Right in the middle of all of this mess, God became a man and dwelt among us. Do you want to know what He did? Good, go read the Gospels[1].

Do you see the difference? It jumps right off the page. Instead of murdering to maintain His position, He humbled Himself. Instead of sacrificing others for Himself, He had compassion on us, sacrificing His life for us. I could go on and on.

By the far the most important history ever, without exception, is the life, death, and resurrection of Jesus. All of the rest of this is

---

1. No seriously, put this book down. I will wait patiently for you to finish.

to help you better understand the Scriptures. The Scriptures speak of Him. Jesus is the complete revelation of God[2]. When you tell people about Jesus[3], I contend you must talk to them about the resurrection of Jesus Christ.

First and foremost, the Resurrection is the Gospel. The problem that unbelievers have is that they suppress the truth in unrighteousness[4]. They know there is a God[5]. They love darkness rather than light because their deeds are evil[6]. Nothing less than the power of God unto salvation[7] is called for if there is to be any hope for their souls.

With the Resurrection as the core of your argument, you can flesh out the Gospel message throughout your conversation. You can talk about why Christ died and His purposes. You can talk about who needs the sacrifice. Most of all you can tell them that it proves the Jesus is God. We can believe everything He told us because He proved that He is the Son of God with power by His resurrection.

Speaking of the Resurrection is also the example left to us in the book of Acts. When is the Gospel presented in the book of Acts when the Resurrection is not mentioned? It is meant to be the proof. It is the one indisputable fact to separate Christ from His rivals.

Uncertainty has no place in a presentation of the Gospel message, and it has no place in a proof of the historical reality of Christ's resurrection. The first reason is that the Scripture commands us to have faith and not to be double minded.

---

2. John 1:18, Colossians 1:15
3. And if you do not, you do not understand the Scriptures at all.
4. Romans 1:18
5. Romans 1:21
6. John 3:19
7. Romans 1:16

Secondly, the evidence for the Resurrection of Jesus Christ is as well established, historically, as it possibly could be. People need to be told the truth and reticence or uncertainty on the part of the one giving the proof is unhelpful and unwarranted. If you are not sure about the facts, how can they be? The Apostles proclaimed the message with all boldness. They can be our example. There is nothing to be unsure about.

Given the methods of history and what it can prove, there is no way for the Resurrection of Christ to be any more evident or certain than it is. Revisionist historians have always used the same methods to attempt to discredit established records. The arguments of those who attempt to dispute the historical reality of Christ's life, death and resurrection reflect nothing more than the ability to cast doubt on anything that happened in the past.

The records of Christ's life were written by those whose lives He changed. Were you expecting the events described to leave people unaffected? The records were maintained by a society whose historians followed His religion. Would you expect people confronted with these powerful historical realities to remain neutral? The accounts of His resurrection were written by His followers. If you witnessed God incarnate risen from the dead, would you not follow Him?

What additional proof could you expect in the situation? The historical record has absolutely everything that you could ask for given the time and location of the events. What do you want, video of the things in question? Video tape would be anachronistic and could be faked in any event. The evidence could not be any surer.

There are three types of religious leaders that have ever been known. There are those who are not real, such as Zeus and Thor. They did all sorts of incredible things. They threw lightning and preformed many supernatural acts. They lived in places that never existed like the mythical Mount Olympus or Asgard and did their deeds at times in the nebulous past that bear no resemblance to any time known to history. This is because they really never existed except in the imagination of their followers. Since they never really existed, they have no power to save their followers.

There are also leaders that were real, such as Mohammed who founded Islam and Siddhartha Gautama, who founded Buddhism. They both lived at real times and in real places. You can learn about their lives, and you can learn about their deaths. Mohammed ate either lamb or goat, depending on the source, which was poisoned. He died. Buddha had some bad pork curry at a ripe old age after much teaching. He also died. Whatever you think of the wisdom or beauty of their teaching is not the point. They cannot save their followers. They could not even save themselves.

Then there is Jesus. He is a real person. He lived in a real place, Roman Judea. He lived at a real time, the First Century AD. He really lived, He really died. He really rose from the dead. He taught some incredible things. He moved through the land banishing sickness and injury. He even brought people back from the dead. He claimed to be God. Since He rose from the dead, we can believe He could do the other miraculous things He is said to have done. We can believe everything He said too.

Some will argue that Jesus Christ is fictitious. He never lived in the first place. There was, they would have you believe, no such man. They argue that accounts of His life are all religious texts and so cannot be considered as evidence. You cannot prove that Jesus rose from the dead unless you can show that He lived in the first place.

First and foremost, the claim that only Christians ever wrote of Christ is entirely false. The Roman historians Suetonius and Tacitus both mention Christ. Both of them were pagans and neither had any love for Christ or Christianity. Neither spoke of

Him for very long but the fact that they mention Him at all is incredible. Both were doing histories of Roman emperors. Rome was to them the center of the world, and Judea of almost no importance except perhaps as the place where Vespasian was stationed before he took power. Very few people from that region are mentioned at all and it is a mark of the importance of Christ and the effect He had that He is noted at all.

Christ was also mentioned by the Jewish historian Josephus. He also would not have been a follower of Christ. He was, however, much more interested in the region of Roman Judea since much of his work was centered there. Josephus mentioned that Christ was persecuted and killed by Pilate. While Josephus was writing after the Jewish insurrection, Jesus was part of the history of the region. This is because He really existed. He is a real person.

From Tacitus, Suetonius and Josephus we also learn about some other real people, like Herod the Great and his incredible cruelty. Pontius Pilate and Agrippa are also mentioned. The political realities are spoken of. All of these details completely confirm the setting of the Biblical accounts of Christ. All these things indeed took place at a real time in a real place. Real things happen in real settings. Things like Christ's real life.

The second thing to point out to this argument about Christ being unreal because only His followers wrote of Him is that the writings of His followers are reliable as historical sources.

First and foremost, they are set in reality. Made up stories feature things that did not happen or places that are not real. If you are familiar with the Gospel accounts, you will find that every miracle and teaching is set in a place; a real place, where you can go today. You can say "I am standing on the hill where Jesus raised the widow's son." "I am in the region of Perea, where Christ taught before He went to Jerusalem to die."

Also note that although there are four accounts of Christ's life, they do not contradict each other. Try getting four witnesses to completely line up their testimony. It is not easy. Now try getting four people, even four that have conspired together, to tell four accounts of the same events even close to the length of the Gospels and see if you can ever get them not to contradict in a thousand ways if their accounts are not true.

Lastly, there are eyewitness details. One example is the eyewitness account of the crucifixion in John. He stated that when Christ's side was pierced, blood and water came out. Medically this is consistent with someone who died because his heart burst. John did not make this up. This medical knowledge was not known in the First Century. He had to witness someone whose heart burst get his side pierced.

It is worth noting that people who died on crosses generally did not die of burst hearts, they died of asphyxiation[8]. John would not have gotten this detail from watching just any crucifixion. Since this knowledge was unknown in the First Century, he also would have had no idea that this detail would show what it does. In other words, there is no reasonable explanation other than that John witnessed Christ getting His side pierced.

Heart failure such as the sort that would result in the blood and water is entirely consistent with the Gospel accounts of Christ's death. Severe agony is a leading cause for such organ failure. Christ experienced the judgment for sin in three hours on the cross.

This argument from the eyewitness account of John has many uses. It establishes the reliability of the Scriptural accounts. It also makes an incredible argument for gratitude and the need to surrender all to follow Christ. It calls for holy living: since Christ

---

8. They couldn't breathe.

suffered this to do away with sin, how can we continue in it? It also is potent in proving that Christ really died.

This leads us to the second thing that had to happen. Jesus had to die. When we say this, it means that He had to die before His resurrection appearances. Nobody disputes the death; it is the timing that is key. Let's look at some of the common objections to the Resurrection.

The objection of the swoon theory, that Jesus was only mostly dead on the cross, not all dead, is easily answered by the points made in the above argument on the reliability of John's eyewitness account of Christ's death. It establishes not only death but time and cause. It becomes unreasonable to contend otherwise. Not that the opposing argument is not already unreasonable. That is, a man who underwent Roman crucifixion managed to roll away a multi-ton boulder and fight his way unarmed through at least eight Roman legionaries after being stabbed with a spear and diagnosed as dead.

I Corinthians 15: 3-4 is clearly an early creed. The fact that Paul quoted it in his letter shows that belief in the Resurrection was established in the church from the beginning. This shows that the contention that the Resurrection occurred was immediate. This is wonderful because of the synergy it has with another argument.

Christianity could have been strangled in its cradle by either the Jews or the Romans if they had just produced Jesus' body and paraded it through the streets. Since we see that belief in the Resurrection is from the beginning integral to the faith, Jewish leaders could have done so and finished off this hated sect. What motivation could they have for not doing so? Compassion? Regret? Or could it be because they could not, no matter how much they would have liked to, because the tomb was empty?

The idea that the disciples could have stolen the body from Roman guards shows an ignorance of history that is remarkable.

Rome ruled the world because of the Roman military. They were well equipped, well trained, disciplined and there were a lot of them. Judean fishermen attacking Roman soldiers would be like bringing a twig to a gunfight. There would have been considerably fewer than twelve disciples after they tried that.

Another weak counter argument to the empty tomb was that it was the wrong tomb. Think about it. The women who anointed Him went to the wrong tomb. The Roman guards were at the wrong tomb. Nobody knew where this tomb was, even after the word spread that He was risen? "Where did I put that tomb hewn from rock into the side of a hill? I just set it down![9] It has to be around here somewhere." Like I said, another weak argument.

You might expect the Roman Empire to weigh in on this and you would be right. Tertullian reported that it was the Roman official's duty to report popular movements to the emperor. When Tiberius received the notification that Jesus had risen from the dead and was consequently looked on as a god, he referred it to the Senate. The Senate cited a Roman law that stated that one could only be a god by vote of the Senate. Since this Jesus did not receive this vote, he could not be recognized by Rome as a god[10].

The most telling argument for the Resurrection is the blood of the disciples. We have records aplenty of people dying for their belief that they had seen Christ risen from the dead. The fact that they believed cannot be reasonably disputed. The fact that their belief was based on their own eyewitness of Christ risen from the grave is the contention in the first place. These are not men who were convinced of the Resurrection by others. If it was not true, each one was in a position to know. There is no record of even one eyewitness saving his life by recanting. We have death by dragging,

---

9. Roman guard patting down his pants like he's feeling for his keys.
10. Not needing their permission, He was God anyway.

crucifixion, clubbing, roasting and spear. If it was a horrible way to die in those days, chances are someone did that instead of recanting. Almost every eyewitness eventually had to make that choice. The conviction of truth could not be stronger, the importance of the belief could not be better established. No other proof could be expected to weather the millennia even remotely so well. It is historically indisputable.

The doubter is forced to resort to mass hallucination or hypnosis. Over five hundred eyes did not see what they thought they saw. They must hang on to this notion despite the fact that not all of them saw Him at the same time, Mass hypnosis at different times and in various locations. Now think about the conversions of James the brother of Jesus and Paul. They did not have any interest in seeing a risen Christ, yet they were both converted by the experience.

How do we know Paul was really converted? Other than manuscript copies of multiple letters he wrote, we have every church in Europe. Paul crossed over into Macedonia and took the Gospel to Europe. Because the Gospel was there it was taken to the Americas. Every time you see a church in either Europe or America you are seeing an effect of the Resurrection of Christ. There is no other cogent explanation for the conversion of Paul.

Another important point that comes out of the earliness of First Corinthians fifteen is that Paul makes the argument that there are over five hundred people who witnessed the resurrection and most of them are still around. The argument "ask anyone, we all saw it" is not consistent with something that did not actually happen.

The conclusion is that given the facts and records that we have, nothing is out of place for the reality of the Resurrection. There is nothing that should be there that is not, neither is there something there that should not be. The situation we find ourselves in is consistent with the Resurrection being a historical fact. In other words, it is consistent with reality. Compare this with the things one is forced to contend to argue against the Resurrection and see how they are fantastic and inconsistent with reality.

Blood of the Martyrs

The death of the Martyrs is the most powerful evidence available of the Resurrection of Christ for those who were not able to witness it themselves. These men gained nothing but toil and a painful death for this testimony in this life. While we have only a handful of accounts of their deaths, we have none of an eyewitness ever recanting.

James the Apostle, brother of John, was beheaded with a sword in Jerusalem at the order of Agrippa. On seeing his calm faith, the first executioner was converted and killed at his side. Philip was tied to a pillar in Hierapolis where he was planting churches and stoned to death. James the son of Alpheus was killed with stones and clubs in Jerusalem when he refused to recant. Barnabas, who had traveled with Paul and sold his land for the poor, was dragged out of the city and burned to death on Cyprus.

With the arrival of Nero there was a great persecution of Christians throughout the empire at his command. He blamed the Christians for a fire his own men set in Rome. Afterwards the Christians in Rome were killed in various ways. Some were thrown to wild animals to entertain crowds. Some were crucified. Others were coated in pitch and used as torches.

Many of the apostles and eyewitnesses of Christ's resurrection were killed at this time rather than recant. Mark was spreading the Gospel in Egypt when he was dragged through the streets of Alexandria but died of the wounds before arriving at the execution site. Peter was crucified upside down after watching his wife executed before his eyes. His wife's suffering was to induce him to recant. Instead, he comforted her. Nero also attempted to get Paul to recant, all in vain. The Apostle went to his death, beheaded by a sword. Paul did not die alone. Soon after Paul was killed, Nero also executed Aristarchus, Epaphras, Prisca, Aquilla, Andronicus and Junia.

When Nero issued his edict against the Christians it became open season on them in Jerusalem. Many of those who were eyewitnesses of the Resurrection were put to death at that time. This persecution did not end with the death of Nero and continued into the reign of Vespasian.

Peter's brother Andrew was crucified at Patras. He hung for three days in which time he was reportedly in good spirits and expressed thanksgiving that he could be of service to God for as long as he had been.

Bartholomew traveled to Armenia where he preached the Gospel converting, among others, the brother of King Astyages. The king had him brought forward and offered him his life if he would renounce Christ and sacrifice to the gods of Armenia. When he refused he was crucified upside down and flayed. From the cross he continued to exhort the people, so his head was removed with an axe.

Thomas, called doubting Thomas by some, disappeared into India where he was killed. The stories of his death are varied and fantastic. Since we have no actual witness accounts, it is impossible to say how it played out.

Matthew went to Ethiopia to serve the fledgling church there. After years of service, a new king came to power who was not a Christian. He had him apprehended while he was teaching, pinned to the ground and beheaded.

Simon the Zealot was apprehended by the governor of Syria. When he would not recant, he too was crucified.

Lastly the Apostle John was exiled to the isle of Patmos rather than recant. With his death the last of the eyewitnesses of the Resurrection passed from this world. Their suffering was harsh to endure. It had the reward that what they said they saw was neither fabrication nor a passing fancy. It was worth dying for. In so doing they laid bedrock evidence for those who came after who were not there to see it for themselves.

19

RELATIONS BETWEEN ROME AND JUDAH

On an appointed day Herod put on his royal robes, took his seat upon the throne, and delivered an oration to them. And the people were shouting, "The voice of a god, and not of a man!" Immediately an angel of the Lord struck him down, because he did not give God the glory, and he was eaten by worms and breathed his last.

During the reign of Herod, anti-Roman rebellion was stifled but did not entirely disappear. After his death, it picked back up and began increasing. Some of this intrigue was military in nature but some was focused on the party of the Pharisees who did not appreciate Herod's Hellenizing influence or his willingness to kowtow to Rome. When Herod required oaths of loyalty, the Pharisees refused consistently to swear loyalty to Herod or Augustus. The followers of two rabbis destroyed an eagle that was in the Temple, which earned their masters' death.

When Herod died, he was out of favor with Rome. His succession was far from ironclad with his heir apparent, Antipater, executed for treason just days before Herod's own death. When Archelaus was acclaimed king by his subjects, he was forced to depart to Rome to receive confirmation. Before he was able to leave, rebellion broke out among the people. The rebellion in Judah and Jerusalem to Roman rule had never really died. The strong rule of Herod the Great had merely caused it to hide out. When Archelaus couldn't remove the High Priest the Hasidim didn't approve of quickly enough, a riot broke out and Archelaus released soldiers to break it up. Three thousand died in the rioting, mostly killed by soldiers.

After the uprising Archelaus left for Rome to have his position sanctioned by Rome. The procurator of Syria, Sabinus, decided he would take custody of Herod's fortresses and treasury. Sabinus was overruled by the Legate Varus who stepped in himself to assure peace in the absence of Archelaus. Varus sent troops into Judea and Jerusalem. Varus showed Roman strength by stationing Roman troops in Jerusalem and judiciously allowed disaffected Jews to send a delegation to Augustus to petition for the removal of Herodian rule. The situation diffused; Varus returned to Syria.

Here again we see the two faces of Roman rule. The efficient, law abiding, peace keeping aspect when it is being represented by just men such as Varus. We also see the corrupt underbelly in the administration of Sabinus. Once Varus was gone, Sabinus installed his troops in the Antonia and attempted to take the treasury in Jerusalem by force of arms. The Jews, whose numbers in Jerusalem were swollen due to Pentecost, fought the Roman soldiers in the streets and cut off the legion from escape.

The anti-Herodian/Roman rebellion became widespread with several revolutions underway simultaneously. Most of these rebellions were more about looting and murdering enemies than political change. In addition to the unrest in Jerusalem, there was Simon, one of Herod's slaves, who set himself up as king of Perea, the land on the other side of the Jordan River that is today part of Jordan. In Idumea, two thousand of Herod's volunteers set up their rule and drew malcontent Jews to their banner. Judas, the son of Ezechias the bandit, continued his father's work by raiding throughout Galilee. In Judea a shepherd named Athronges set himself up as king and began punishing the pro-Roman and Herodian partisans. He and his brothers set about a murder spree that extended to ambushing a Roman Century near Emmaus. The army of Herod was completely unable to deal with the situation and lawlessness reigned in Judah.

Varus returned at the head of Roman legions. The rebellions dissipated in the face of the arrival of real authority. Varus relieved Sabinus and sent the captured ringleaders to Rome for punishment. He then made an example by crucifying two thousand rebels outside Jerusalem. The power of Rome again proved irresistible, and the rebellion of Judah was quelled.

The crown was withheld from Archelaus, and he was given instead the region of Judea, with Antipas receiving Galilee and Philip receiving largely gentile regions. When Archelaus was removed from office and exiled to Gaul, Judea was annexed as a Roman Province. The independence of Judea was no longer extant even in name. The move to provincial status brought about a new per head tax. This was the tax that Jesus was asked if it was lawful to pay. This tax rankled many Jews and opposition to Roman rule, and the rebellion it would bring, crystallized against this new imposition.

This new brand of Judaism was similar to that of the Pharisees but while the Pharisee was content if he could observe the Law of Moses in freedom, these rebels began to demand that Jews must be under no master but God. This new faction was willing to risk anything for freedom. This was the beginning of what would eventually become the Zealots.

Meanwhile Herod Antipas, the Tetrarch of Galilee, had married the daughter of Aretas, king of the Arabs living in Petra. Remember that because it will cause trouble later. What really caused trouble was that Herod Antipas, while staying at his half-brother Herod Philip's[1] house, decided that he preferred Herod Philip's wife, Herodias, to his own wife, the daughter of King Aretas. More on these guys later.

When Pontius Pilate was appointed procurator of Judea, he made the mistake of having his troops bear standards with images of Caesar when he entered Jerusalem. Despite the uproar from the people, he set up the images in Jerusalem and retired to Caesarea. A crowd of Jews arrived and entreated him to take them down. Pilate felt that it would dishonor Caesar to do so. When they insisted, he threatened to have the soldiers kill them. When the Jews accepted his terms if only he would remove the images, Pilate backed down. These Jews were intense.

Hopefully you recognize some of the names you have been seeing. From Herod the Great, who murdered the children of Bethlehem like he did his own, to Pontius Pilate, Jesus of Nazareth was living His life. God Incarnate walked the earth as that history was taking place. Jesus has His own chapter in this book. It isn't intended to replace the Gospels. There is no need to add anything there. You have the primary source, go read it. The chapter on Jesus is about historical arguments that surround Him and the importance of the historical reality of His life, death, and resurrection.

Meanwhile in Rome, Agrippa, the son of Aristobulus[2] was

---

1. Not Philip the Tetrarch, the other one.
2. One of the two brothers that Herod killed.

living large. His mother Bernice disapproved of his profligate spending habits, but that didn't stop him. One of his main problems was that he liked to give big gifts. When his mother died, his generosity left him in poverty.

He fled to Judea in shame ahead of his creditors. When he decided to stay with his sister Herodias, he received a position as a magistrate at Tiberius as a gift from his brother-in-law Herod Antipas[3]. The situation fell apart when Herod Antipas flung Agrippa's poverty in his face when they were both drunk at a party.

At this juncture, Agrippa tried to return to Rome. There was some difficulty since he owed important people money, important people who were able to throw him in jail. It was trailing the demands of creditors that Agrippa threw himself on the mercy of Tiberius Caesar. Tiberius refused to associate with him until he had paid his debts. Agrippa managed to sting someone else for a loan way larger than he needed for his debts and used the rest to make spectacular gifts to Gaius Caesar.

Agrippa and Gaius were fast friends and went chariot riding together. One day he remarked that it would be wonderful if Tiberius were to kick off so Gaius could be emperor. When Tiberius heard this from a servant who had been stealing and decided to change the subject by snitching on Agrippa, he went off. Immediately Agrippa was placed in chains and made to wander about the palace still wearing his royal garments.

In Judea, King Aretas's daughter, fresh from being cast off by Herod Antipas for Herodias, went back to daddy complaining. Aretas gathered his army and met Herod Antipas' army in open battle. The slaughter of Herod Antipas' army was seen by locals as

---

3. Herodias and Herod Antipas are the ones who chopped off John the Baptist's head.

judgment for having John the Baptist put to death after throwing him in the prison Macherus.

The Roman army forced Aretas' men to withdraw. Before Tiberius Caesar could punish Aretas for breaking the peace, word arrived that Tiberius had died and been replaced by Gaius Caesar. The Roman general had to await word to know if he was still to take out Aretas as Tiberius had wanted.

If Aretas was happy about this turn of events, it couldn't hold a candle to Agrippa's joy. Gaius replaced his iron chain with one of gold. He made him king of Philip's Tetrarchy. Agrippa returned to Judea to strut about and display his new magnificence. After he had his fill of lording it over the locals, he returned to Rome to live. What was wealth for if it wasn't giving extravagant parties for your best bud the Emperor of Rome? You can't do that from Judea.

Herodias was less than pleased by her brother's good fortune. The ungrateful little snot had mooched off of them and then ran off with his pants in a knot. She had been waiting for him to come crawling back. Now he was swanking about in royal dignity while her husband was just the Tetrarch of Galilee. It burned her. She began nagging Herod Antipas to go get a kingdom too. He tried to ignore her, but she kept on until he agreed to go see Gaius just for a moment's peace.

They were in the presence petitioning when word arrived from Agrippa that Herod Antipas was plotting treasonous actions against Rome with the Parthians. That settled it; Herod Antipas and Herodias were exiled for the rest of their lives to Gaul. Agrippa got to add Galilee and Perea to his kingdom.

Matters took a serious turn for the worse when Gaius Caesar, known as the infamous Caligula, decided to abandon sanity. He implied that he was not only a god but perhaps even the most important one. He had temples throughout the empire take their statues and send them to his palace. He ordered that a bridge be built over a bay so he could ride his chariot over the water. He threatened to make his horse a Consul. You get the picture.

The import of this change in conduct was that Caligula ordered that a statue of himself in the role of Jupiter be installed in the Temple for worship. While things had not been uniformly smooth between Rome and Judah since the annexation, this edict was sure to cause rebellion in even the most placid Jews. The governor of Syria was ordered, despite his pleas, to take two Roman legions to enforce the placing of the statue.

Meanwhile in Rome, Agrippa was giving one of his over-the-top parties for Caligula. Caligula was most conscious of who his best friend was. Agrippa gave the best parties and nobody else was close. Where did he even get the money for these things? Caligula decided to express his pleasure by inviting Agrippa to ask him for anything and he would give it to him. Agrippa replied that he already had more than he ever could have hoped for from Caligula in his friendship. Caligula countered that he could ask for anything, he was serious. Just do it. Agrippa said he couldn't. Gaius told him "Do it!" Agrippa responded that, well, there was one little thing Caligula could do for his people. Perhaps, if it wasn't too much trouble, he could refrain from crushing their spirits by placing a statue of himself in the Temple.

Agrippa knew he was playing with fire. This was Caligula and Agrippa knew very well what he had become. Asking for this could have easily meant the end of not only his royal dignity but also his life. The gamble paid off, and the statue thing was at least put off.

The Judeans were not the only people to not be enjoying this new sort of maniacal emperor. A group of men who were responsible for his guard and some senators decided to strike for freedom by punching a bunch of sword shaped holes in Caligula as he was going from the theater to the bath. There was some anarchy, and Claudius ended up being hailed as Emperor by the legions. The senators were of the opinion that they were free men once more now that the emperor was dead.

Agrippa got Caligula's body and called for a medic. After he was confirmed as dead, Agrippa openly mourned for him, even though the opinion on the street was that Caligula had it coming. When the Senate, many of whom were directly responsible for the murder, asked him for advice on what to do in the situation, Agrippa advised them not to try fighting the legions and accept Claudius as Emperor.

Claudius restored to Agrippa the kingdom of Herod the Great. He also, on Agrippa's request, made Agrippa's brother Herod[4] king of Chalcis[5].

Claudius had been good to Agrippa, but he wasn't his close friend Gaius. There was really nothing keeping Agrippa in Rome now. He returned to Judah to rule his kingdom in style. He offered the sacrifices that were fitting for the king. One day when he was hosting the games in honor of Caesar, Agrippa addressed the multitudes while dressed in a silver garment. It wasn't a silver-colored garment. No, this garment was made of actual silver. As the morning light shone from his magnificent get up, the people cried out that he was more like a god than a man. Almost immediately, he began to suffer from stomach pain. It was only a few days before Judah was once more without a king.

While the monarchy was revived briefly under Agrippa, Judah became a Roman province again after his death. The Proconsuls sent from Rome began to see rebellions rise in the aftermath of the dissolution of monarchy. After this point, the peace in the

---

4. Yes, another Herod. At this point it's just funny.
5. A bit of Syria north of Israel.

province broke down until the final destruction of Judah through the razing of Jerusalem.

The rebellions began in earnest with the Roman procurator Cumanus. A number of incidents set the stage for the deterioration of relations between Rome and Judah. First a Roman soldier exposed himself during Passover. The Jews felt he was doing it to taunt God rather than themselves. This led to angry crowds being stampeded out of the Temple, resulting in trampling deaths.

Later, when an imperial slave was murdered by a lawless band, a member of the punitive force sent out to punish the brigands took it upon himself to take a law scroll from a synagogue, rip it across and burn it. Cumanus had the soldier publicly beheaded. The worst incident resulted when Samaritans attacked and murdered Galilean pilgrims. When Cumanus refused to act, the pro-Zealot rebels organized bands and blazed a path through several Samaritan villages. Cumanus then used Roman troops to put down the Galilean and Judean forces. The Legate of Syria, Quadratus, had to intervene. He executed people on both sides and sent others to Rome for trial. He also relieved Cumanus of his position and returned him in disgrace to Rome.

Felix was appointed procurator of Judea from Rome. The next year Agrippa's son Agrippa II had to give up his Tetrarchy of Chalcis but was made king of the Tetrarchy of Philip[6]. His sister Drusilla married Felix. On the death of Claudius, Nero also gave Galilee and Tiberias to Agrippa.

---

6. If you recall he had some land northeast of the Sea of Galilee.

20

ROME AND JUDAH DURING THE TIME OF THE EARLY CHURCH

And when he drew near and saw the city, he wept over it, saying, "Would that you, even you, had known on this day the things that make for peace! But now they are hidden from your eyes. For the days will come upon you, when your enemies will set up a barricade around you and surround you and hem you in on every side and tear you down to the ground, you and your children within you. And they will not leave one stone upon another in you, because you did not know the time of your visitation."

On the death of Procurator Porcius Festus, Albinus was appointed to replace him. Before the new procurator could arrive, Ananus the High Priest and the Pharisees convened the Sanhedrin against James, the brother of Jesus and other Christians in Jerusalem. Ananus was punished by

Albinus for what he did, but it was little comfort for the Christians of Jerusalem who had been stoned.

After this the peace of Rome was disturbed frequently by armed bands of Zealot terrorists raiding the countryside. They would loot the estates of collaborators and villages that refused to aid their anti-Roman politics. Another difficulty was the profusion of false messiahs that abounded during this time. Large crowds would be gathered to aid the messiah in taking Jerusalem and booting out Rome. Naturally Roman forces were used to break up these gatherings. The anti-Roman factions also adopted the use of dagger men who blended into crowds and murdered their victims with concealed daggers. The ex-High Priest Jonathan was their first victim.

Increasingly, Rome was unable to control the lawlessness in the countryside and the corrupt infighting inside Jerusalem. Open revolt broke out in 66 AD over ethnic hatreds between Jews and Greeks in Caesarea. The problems were compounded when the Roman Procurator Florus demanded money from the Temple treasury. Some Jews took a collection for coppers for the "indigent procurator" and when the Sanhedrin refused to hand them over or identify the ones who did the collection, Florus released his cohort of troops to sack the upper city of Jerusalem. They went on a spree of devastation and murder and Florus had their prisoners scourged and crucified. Two further cohorts arrived with the result of Roman forces being besieged in various fortresses in Jerusalem surrounded by angry rebel forces. Florus was forced to flee, and Agrippa II arrived and prevented violence for a short while. After Agrippa left, dagger men took the Masada and massacred the Roman garrison. The final rebellion against Rome had begun.

The first reprisals from Rome came from Gallus, the Legate of Syria. He brought a force of thirty thousand through Galilee, subduing it. He then continued to Jerusalem, setting fire to Lydda. Gallus led a short assault on the walls of Jerusalem and then, inexplicably, withdrew. The Jews harried his retreat and he lost six thousand Roman soldiers. Jerusalem had its independence, but the loss of soldiers ensured that Rome would be back to make an example of them. Once you let anyone have freedom, keeping the empire together becomes ten times as hard.

The rebels in Judah spent a great deal of time fighting among themselves, particularly when Roman forces were not threatening. The city of Jerusalem itself was divided between rival camps. By all rights, Judah should have fallen immediately. With the withdrawal of Gallus, Judah had a brief interlude of independence before the nation would be blotted out until the Twentieth Century. With the overwhelming power of Rome, it is unlikely unity would have helped them anyhow.

With the death of Gallus, Nero appointed Vespasian to reduce the Jewish regions. Vespasian brought his son, Titus, as second in command. He also brought sixty thousand men including three Roman legions. From 67 to 68 AD Vespasian took Galilee and the area surrounding Jerusalem. He carefully reduced Judean fortresses through siege and took the ports from insurgent hands as well. He arranged his legions around Jerusalem and prepared camps for the siege. Before the assault, Vespasian received word that Nero had died. His mandate to take Jerusalem was at an end.

While Vespasian did maintain control of the region, he preferred to let the factions inside Jerusalem wear each other down. Vespasian left command of the assault with his son when he returned to Rome to take his place as emperor. Titus added a legion to the number and picked up the siege of Jerusalem in 70 AD.

The inhabitants of Jerusalem proved resistant to both the horrific famine that the siege brought on and the psychological fear that Titus used by parading Roman forces around the walls. In the end Titus used earthworks and siege equipment to break through the northern walls. Here again a Roman army smashed into Jerusalem and entered through the Temple wall. The Temple porticos were fired, and Roman forces were released to kill and loot. The Temple itself was not spared and it was burned and looted. Roman legions made sacrifices to their standards there.

Titus reserved the handsomest of the survivors for his triumph. The men were sent to slavery in mines or gladiatorial shows. The children were enslaved. The old were butchered. The city of Jerusalem was destroyed. So ended the nation of Judah. Judah had placed itself under Rome through the petitions of Hyrcanus and Alexander. Rome had held power over them sometimes fairly and other times corruptly but always working to preserve the peace and order of the empire. The Jews were rebellious, some because they had nationalistic pride and others due to the religious belief that only Jews or God should rule them. The disorder of their rebellion and the high-handed way in which Rome protected the peace and suffered no resistance led to the relatively swift destruction of the nation of Judah under Roman rule. In the rest of the empire, where their zeal for the Law of Moses led more to moral actions than sedition, Jews fared better.

The Spread of the Gospel in the Days Following the Resurrection

As I mentioned as we approached the life of our Lord and Savior, this book is not about telling you what you can easily read in the Bible. In this case the book in question is Acts. That book is historical in nature and tracks the progress of the Gospel from an upper room in Jerusalem as it is driven by the Holy Spirit throughout the Roman world. If you are not familiar with that account, I urge you to read it. My goal in this section is to first enhance the accounts of the ministries of Peter and Paul recorded in Acts with background information and then talk about what we know about the spread of the Gospel in directions not spoken of in Acts.

After persecution forced many of the Christians living in Jerusalem to scatter, we read that they went their way preaching the Gospel. What was that Gospel? It was that Jesus was the Messiah and He had come offering salvation. It was that even though He had been crucified, He had risen from the dead, even as He had said He would. It was a message borne by Jews and preached primarily to Jews. There are some notable exceptions, such as the Ethiopian eunuch and the Samaritans. At first though the church was overwhelmingly Jewish.

One place of particular note where the Gospel bore great fruit was Syrian Antioch. It was a city that was very much involved in the growth and friction associated with the drawing of Gentiles into the church in large numbers. The first thing you should know if you do not already is that there are multiple Antiochs, two of which are spoken of in Scripture. The one that concerns us here is Syrian Antioch which is today in far southern Turkey by the Orontes River just a few miles from the border with Syria. The other one, Pisidian Antioch, is considerably farther west in central Turkey and is an entirely different kettle of fish.

The reason we have multiple cities named Antioch is because of the Seleucid kingdom. More of their rulers were named Antiochus than Seleucius even though the latter was the name of the dynasty. Syrian Antioch was founded by Seleucius I and named for his father. It was one of four cities he built at that time in a square they called the Tetropolis. He filled it with a mixture of Greeks and Hellenized Jews. Of the four cities, Antioch was set up to be the one that would be most defensible. It was built by a river and a mountain in a location that would be difficult to attack. It was set up close to the enemies of the west such as Rome and Hellenic successor states to Alexander's conquests. From this fortified city, the Seleucid Empire could stage its campaigns.

As it panned out, Antioch became the capitol of the Seleucid Empire. Goods from Persia came through there on their way west. The goods that traveled along the route originated as far away as China on a trade route known today as the Silk Road. As time passed successive emperors added further sections to the city as it grew in importance both in the empire and internationally. Even after Syria was nothing more than a Roman province, Antioch was a city of major importance in the region. Until the construction of Constantinople, Antioch was the third largest city in the Roman Empire behind only Alexandria in Egypt and Rome itself.

Just southwest of Antioch there was a beautiful grove of trees with fountains and statues that were to honor Daphne and Apollo. It was placed there at the same time as the city and was entirely associated with it. People would come from all around to engage in immorality at the festivals held there. Once the Gospel reached Antioch, it took hold in a major way, so much so that afterwards it had a reputation as a particularly Christian city.

It was in Syrian Antioch that the church laid hands on Paul and sent him out as a missionary. Consequently, this city's sending church was used to bring the Gospel to Asia Minor and Macedonia. Paul also claims to have preached the Gospel as far as Illyricum which would be as far as modern day Albania. It is clear from the book of Romans that the Gospel reached the empire's capitol through other means than Paul and his sending church of Antioch.

Colossae / Laodicea / Hierapolis

Colossae was one hundred miles east of Ephesus in Asia Minor. It was located in a narrow part of the Lycus River valley next to Mount Cadmus. Stone could be mined in the mountain and there was a fine cold-water spring. It had a large and cosmopolitan population. Colossae was famous for the black wool from its local sheep. Where once it was a major trade hub, by Roman times it was too far off of the main roads and was in decline. The roads had moved the trade to nearby Laodicea.

Laodicea was in its prime during the First Century. The trade routes allowed it to make fortunes in trade and banking. The black wool of the local sheep moved just as well there as it had at Colossae. Laodicea, while rich, had no water supply so had to depend on aqueducts to bring water from Colossae and Hierapolis. By the time the water arrived, both the cold and hot waters were just lukewarm. Rich and lukewarm, just like certain churches I could mention.

Hierapolis also prospered after the decline of Colossae. The local hot springs were a major factor in that rise. The wealthy have always found bathing in hot springs health giving. At the very least, it was luxurious.

The church at Colossae was not on Paul's itinerary and had been planted by Epaphras, a believer who had been converted during Paul's stay in Ephesus. Paul wrote his letter to this city during his second imprisonment in 60 AD. He also wrote letters at the same time for Laodicea and a personal one for Philemon, who lived in Colossae. There was a sizable Jewish population in Colossae since Antiochus III settled a couple thousand Jews there about 200 BC.

The city was also home to the cult of Cybele. Cybele was an adaptation of an Anatolian fertility goddess that made it into the

Roman pantheon. Augustus looked on her as a goddess of Troy[1]. Her worship was somewhat mysterious since, as a mystery religion, those who were not part of the cult were not allowed to know what was going on. What we do know is quite enough. Her priests were men who castrated themselves to offer up their fertility to Cybele. The priests stood under a grate where a sacrifice was being made. They would be doused by the blood of a cow as it was drained and then drink its milk afterwards. The priests had to subsist on what they could beg. At the same time there are also records of wild ecstatic marches through the streets during the festivals. This was a religion that depended on experience to generate a feeling of connection to the divine. It was accomplished through excess and asceticism[2].

The result of these schools of thought mixing resulted in some dualistic philosophy. This school of thought believed that God, being perfect, could not have created the evil world of flesh. He must have created some demi-gods that created the physical world. Dualists strove to become more spiritual and less fleshly in order to make themselves appealing to God. They would deny themselves, or practice asceticism. Imagine their trouble understanding when Epaphras showed up with the Gospel and declared that God became flesh and rose from the dead.

Corinth

Corinth was one of the most populous and wealthy cities of the Roman era. It is located on a narrow stretch of land[3] that connects mainland Greece with the Peloponnese. Not only did this put

---

1. The Romans believed that the city was founded by refugees from the Trojan War who settled in Italy.
2. Denying yourself things, particularly food and other necessities.
3. It's called an isthmus.

Corinth smack dab in the middle of trade between the two regions of Greece, but it held a strategic position for sea trade as well. The Peloponnese is not a tiny peninsula. It was worth the time of merchants to unload on one side, haul their cargo to the other side and load on new ships. It was kind of like the Panama Canal only it didn't have a canal yet.

You might hear about the legendary immorality of Corinth. Corinth was not a moral city, but the legendary accounts of immorality were attributed to Greek Corinth. Greek Corinth was destroyed by Rome in 146 BC. A century later in 44 BC, Julius Caesar founded Roman Corinth.

This means it was a Roman city. The people of Corinth had full Roman citizenship with all of the rights that brought. It was the capitol of Roman Achaia. The Roman Proconsul lived there. While the city had abundant Greek culture as well, it was decidedly more Roman than most of its neighbors.

Ephesus

Ephesus in New Testament times was under the rule of the Roman Empire. It was very important because it had the main port of entry into the Roman province of Asia, known today as Turkey. From Ephesus, roads traveled throughout Asia and further inland. This allowed the people of Ephesus to thrive from trade as goods flowed through their port.

The port of Ephesus was by the Mediterranean Sea. All of the territories that bordered this sea, Southern Europe, Northern Africa and Western Asia, were under the dominion of Rome at this time. Because of this, ports on the Mediterranean connected a city to all of the trade of the Roman Empire.

Because of this port, Ephesus was very important and prosperous, both in New Testament times and a thousand years prior.

Because it was the main port the roads from all of the other cities were large and much traffic passed over them. This meant that in addition to money, Ephesus was important because it was well connected with the other cities with constant flow of culture and information between Ephesus and its neighbors.

The other main reason why Ephesus was important among the cities of Asia Minor was that it was the home of the Temple of Diana. By the time of the New Testament, that was the largest building in the Greek speaking world and was counted as one of the seven wonders of the ancient world. Ephesus also had three temples to Roman emperors that were worshiped as gods.

The "Diana" or "Artemis" of Ephesus was not the same as the one you hear about in your classical Greek mythology. While the Artemis of mythology was a huntress that was forever a virgin, the "Artemis" of Ephesus had once been a native fertility goddess of the Anatolian region. The culture of the region was closely related to the areas of the Near East, the regions that today make up Iran and Iraq. In these places, fertility goddesses were worshiped by engaging in sexual immorality with prostitutes in the temple. Despite the name change when the city was influenced by Greek culture, the nature of the goddess "Artemis" of the Ephesians was the same as it had been before the name change.

The Temple of Diana was the center of idol worship of that false goddess in the region. To make matters even worse, the temple of Diana was also a place known for the practice of magic and people paid well for the spells practiced there. This caused Ephesus to be both a center of this vile religion and a center of culture in the region as people came from all over the Roman world. This only served to increase the importance that Ephesus had in the region.

Ephesus had been an Anatolian settlement when in about 1000 BC Ionian Greeks arrived and settled in the city. About 560

BC Croesus conquered Ephesus and built it up and beautified it with art. After Croesus fell, the city fell into the hands of the Persian Empire. It fell to Alexander the Great, along with the rest of the Persian Empire and was part of the territories of Lysomachus when Alexander's kingdom was divided on his death. In 133 BC it was left to Rome in the will of the king of Pergamon and became part of the Roman Empire. The population was about three hundred thousand at its height, the largest city in the region.

The Apostle Paul came to Ephesus at the end of his second missionary journey and founded a church there. His ministry there can be found in the nineteenth chapter of Acts. He taught there for two years and left Priscilla and Aquila there when he left. Paul was very close to the church in Ephesus and visited the elders despite the threat to his life. It is believed that he wrote the Epistle to the Ephesians from prison in Rome.

The Gospel is believed to have spread to the nearby cities in Asia Minor from the Ephesian church. The centrality of Ephesus and many roads made it possible for the believers to travel throughout the region to spread the Gospel. Later at about 90 AD the Apostle John sent letters to seven churches in the region, the first being Ephesus. These letters, found in the second chapter of "The Revelation of Jesus Christ" find the Ephesian church doctrinally sound and alert for false teachers but lacking in love.

Believers in Ephesus faced challenges to living righteously because of the pagan culture of idol worship and magic. There was no more immoral city in Asia Minor. The people saved out of this society would need guidance in how to live a life that pleased God. In addition to teaching faithfully for two years, Paul also decided to write them a letter to give them instructions on how to live for God in an immoral society.

It is also believed that the Epistle to the Ephesians was meant to be sent throughout the region of Asia. This is because some ancient manuscripts lack the words translated "In Ephesus." The instructions would be valuable to other cities in the region just as it is valuable to us today. Whether this theory is true or not, the other cities in Asia did get copies of the letter to the Ephesians to read and the words of this epistle were quickly used throughout the Christian church and regarded as Scripture.

Galatia

This is a region of the Roman Empire in modern day Turkey as opposed to a specific city. Back then it was Asia Minor. It includes the modern city of Ankara, the capital of Turkey. The Bible cities in the region you might have read about are Iconium, Derbe and Pisidian Antioch.

Philippi

Named after Philip of Macedon, this city overlooks plains in northern Macedonia. It is sixteen miles from the coast and lies along a major road from Rome to Asia Minor. Its location was selected for its defensibility as a citadel to protect the surrounding lands.

A major battle was fought in its vicinity in which Marc Antony and Octavian finished off Brutus and Cassius. In celebration the city was "refounded" as a Roman city. As you might have guessed, there was Roman citizenship for everybody. In order to increase the Roman character of the city, retiring veterans were settled there by the victorious generals.

Thessalonica

Thessalonica was the most important city in Macedonia. Unlike most ancient cities, it has continued to be inhabited since its founding. It was initially named Therma but was renamed after the sister of Alexander the Great and wife of Cassander. The city lies along the Roman highway that connected Rome to Asia Minor and the East. As a result, it flourished from trade.

There is an interesting story associated with the name. When Phillip, Alexander's father, managed to make an advantageous marriage, it gave him control of the region of Thessaly. When a daughter was born of this union, he named her " Victory in Thessaly," or Thessalonica.

It was made the capital of Roman Macedonia under Antony and granted its citizenship in 41 BC. As time went by it became the administrative capital of all Greece for Rome. In the First Century AD it was visited by Paul the Apostle and became a center for Christianity.

WITH THE REVELATION to John the Cannon closed. At the close of the First Century, Christianity was still an illegal religion in the Roman Empire. How the Gospel overcame Rome and spread throughout the world is an entirely different history. A history that will have to be the subject of another book.

What I can tell you is that faithful men and women followed Christ's example by making disciples and teaching them. Generation after generation the faith has been passed on in this way. Nobody knows the day or the hour, but the story does not end until Christ returns. It is for us to make disciples and teach them until then.

BIBLIOGRAPHY

Aharoni, Yohannan. *The Land of the Bible: A Historical Geography.* Translated by A.F. Rainey. Philadelphia, PA: The Westminster Press, 1967.

Albright, W.F. *The Archeology of Palestine: A Survey of the Ancient Peoples and Cultures of the Holy Land.* London, UK: Penguin Books LTD, 1949.

Alt, Albrecht. *Essays on Old Testament History and Religion.* Translated by R. A. Wilson. Garden City, NY: Doubleday, 1967.

Ashton, John and Down, David. *Unwrapping the Pharaohs: How Egyptian Archeology Confirms the Biblical Timeline.* Green Forest, AR: Master Books, 2006.

Avi-Yanah, Michael, ed. *Encyclopedia of Archeological Excavations in the Holy Land.* Englewood Cliffs, NJ: Prentice Hall, 1975.

Ben-Tor, Amnon. *The Archeology of Ancient Israel.* Translated by R. Greenberg. London, UK: Yale University Press, 1992.

Braudel, Fernand. *The Mediterranean and the Mediterranean World in the Age of Phillip II: Volume I.* Translated by Sian Reynolds. New York, NY: Harper and Rowe, 1973.

Braudel, Fernand. *The Mediterranean and the Mediterranean World in the Age of Phillip II: Volume II.* Translated by Sian Reynolds. New York, NY: Harper and Rowe, 1973.

Bruce, F.F. *Israel and the Nations: From the Exodus to the Fall of the Second Temple.* Grand Rapids, MI: Wm. B. Eerdmans Publishing Company, 1963.

Callaway, Joseph. "The Settlement in Canaan: The period of the Judges" revised by J. Maxwell Miller. In *Ancient Israel: From Abraham to the Roman Destruction of the Temple,* ed. Herschel Shanks, pp. 55-90. Washington, DC: Biblical Archeology Society; Upper Saddle River, NJ: Prentice Hall, 1999.

Castel, Francois. *The History of Israel and Judah in Old Testament Times.* Translated by Matthew O'Connell. Mahwah, NJ: Paulist Press, 1983.

Duncan, J. Garrow. *Digging up Biblical History: Recent Archeology in Palestine and its Bearing on The Old Testament Historical Narratives.* New York, NY: The Macmillan Co., 1931.

Gabriel, Richard A. *The Military History of Ancient Israel.* Westport, CT: Praeger, 2003.

Goodman, Martin. *Rome and Jerusalem: The Clash of Ancient Civilizations.* New York, NY: Alfred A Knopf, 2007.

Grant, Michael. *The Jews in the Roman World.* New York, NY: Charles Scribner's Sons, 1973.

Greenspoon, Leonard J. *Textual Studies in the Book of Joshua*. Chico, CA: Scholars Press, 1983.

Grayzel, Solomon. *A History of the Jews*. Philadelphia, PA: The Jewish Publication Society of America, 1947.

Hermann, Siegfried. *A History of Israel in Old Testament Times*. Philadelphia: Fortress Press, 1975.

Hester, H.I. *The Heart of Hebrew History: A Study of the Old Testament*. Liberty, MO: The Quality Press, Inc., 1963.

Isserlin, B.S.J. *The Israelites*. London, UK: Thames and Hudson, 1998.

Johnson, Paul A. *A History of the Jews*. New York, NY: Harper & Rowe, 1987.

Jones, Dr. Floyd Nolen. *The Chronology of the Old Testament: A Return to the Basics*. Green Forest, AR: Master Books, 2005.

Josephus, Flavius. *The New Complete Works of Josephus*. Translated by William Whiston. Grand Rapids, MI: Kregel, 1999.

Kaiser, Walter C. *A History of Israel: From the Bronze Age Through the Jewish Wars*. Nashville, TN: Broadman and Holman Publishers, 1998.

Kitchen, K.A. *On The Reliability of the Old Testament*. Grand Rapids, MI: Wm. B. Eerdmans Publishing Company, 2003.

Kitto, John. *Palestine: From the Patriarchal Age to the Present Time*. New York, NY: Peter Fenlon Collier, 1851.

Learsi, Rufus. *Israel: A History of the Jewish People*. Westport, CT: Greenwood Press, 1949.

Linder, Amnon. *The Jews in Imperial Roman Legislation*. Detroit MI, Wayne State University Press, 1987.

MacAlister, Robert. *A History of Civilization in Palestine*. London, UK: Cambridge, 1912.

Margolis, Max L. and Marx, Alexander. *A History of the Jewish People*. Philadelphia, PA: The Jewish Publication Society of America, 1927.

Merrill, Eugene H. *Kingdom of Priests: A History of Old Testament Israel*. Grand Rapids, MI: Baker Academics, 2008.

Miller, J. Maxwell and Hayes, John H. *A History of Ancient Israel and Judah*. Louisville, KY: Westminster John Knox Press, 2006.

Mospero, G. *History of Egypt: Volume II*. Translated by M. L. McClure. London, UK: William Clowes and Sons, 1905.

Mospero, G. *History of Egypt: Volume IV*. Translated by M. L. McClure. London, UK: William Clowes and Sons, 1905.

Mospero, G. *History of Egypt: Volume V*. Translated by M. L. McClure. London, UK: William Clowes and Sons, 1905.

Noth, Martin. *The History of Israel*. Translated by Stanley Godman. New York, NY: Harper & Brothers, 1958.

Noth, Martin. *The Old Testament World*. Translated by Victor I Gruhn. Philadelphia, PA: Fortress Press, 1966.

Polzin, Robert. *Samuel and the Deuteronomist: Part II*. San Francisco, CA: Harper & Rowe, 1989.

Price, Ira Maurice, Sellers, Ovid and Carlson, E. Leslie. *The Monuments and the Old Testament*. Philadelphia, PA: The Judson Press, 1958.

Ricciotti, Giuseppe. *The History of Israel: From the Beginning to the Exile*. Translated by Clement Penta and Richard Murphy. Milwaukee, WI: Bruce Publishing, 1955.

Robinson, George Livingstone. *The Bearing of Archeology on the Old Testament*. New York, NY: American Tract Society, 1941.

Routledge, Bruce. *Moab in the Iron age: Hegemony, Polity, Archeology*. Philadelphia, PA: University of Pennsylvania Press, 2004.

Sailhamer, John. *Genesis Unbound*. Colorado Springs, CO: Dawson Media, 2011.

Sarna, Nahum. "Israel in Egypt: The Egyptian Sojourn and the Exodus" revised by Herschel Shanks. In *Ancient Israel: From Abraham to the Roman Destruction of the Temple,* ed. Herschel Shanks, pp. 33-54. Washington, DC: Biblical Archeology Society; Upper Saddle River, NJ: Prentice Hall, 1999.

Smallwood, E. Mary. *The Jews under Roman Rule: From Pompey to Diocletian*. Leiden, Netherlands: E. J. Brill, 1981.

Suetonius, Gaius. *The Twelve Caesars*. London, UK: Penguin, 1957.

Tacitus, Publius Cornelius. *The Annals of Imperial Rome*. Translated by Michael Grant. New York, NY: Penguin, 1971.

Thiele, Edwin. *The Mysterious Numbers of the Hebrew Kings*. New York, NY: Macmillan, 1951.

Thompson, Thomas L. *The Mythic Past: Biblical Archeology and the Myth of Israel*. London, UK: Random House, 1999.

Thucydides. *The History of the Peloponnesian War*. Translated by Rex Warner. London, UK: Penguin Classics, 1972.

Van De Mieroop, Marc. *A History of Ancient Egypt*. Malden, MA: Blackwell Publishing, 2011.

Van De Mieroop, Marc. *A History of the Ancient Near East*. Malden, MA: Blackwell Publishing, 2007.

ABOUT THE AUTHOR

Dennis Troyer has been serving middle school students as a teacher and youth minister for over twenty years. He is married to Stephanie and has been blessed with three amazing daughters, Rachel, Rosie and Ruth Ellen. He has a bachelor's from the University of Texas, San Antonio in History and a master's in Biblical Studies from the Master's University.

When he has spare time, he likes to write.

www.ingramcontent.com/pod-product-compliance
Lightning Source LLC
Chambersburg PA
CBHW050859160426
43194CB00011B/2211